Born to Rumble

Speedway fights, fracas,
barneys, banter and bust ups

Jeff Scott

methanol
press

In memory of my mum, Mary

Always my proudest reader

First published in Great Britain by
Methanol Press
2 Tidy Street Brighton East Sussex BN1 4EL

For a complete catalogue of current and forthcoming publications please write to the address above, or visit our website at www.methanolpress.com

ISBN 978-0-9568618-4-9

A catalogue for this book is available from the British Library

Editor in absentia: Michael Payne
Word Wrangler: Graham Russel
Book & Cover Design: Vicky Holtham

Printed in the UK

Chapter One – Belle Vue

....

I arrive very early at Kirkmanshulme Lane, and enjoy a long, pleasant conversation with Belle Vue promoter Ian Thomas. After the initial misstep of our first encounter on a busy televised race night, I've been very touched by Ian's generosity and help on many occasions. This afternoon is no exception since a brief glance in the match programme for this evening's fixture reveals that there is a full-page article on my book in the programme by the esteemed journalist and gifted speedway ghost-writer Richard Frost. He's very complimentary about my book, though he also gently takes the mickey and makes the odd pointed aside. I'm absolutely made up with the coverage and also appreciate his humour.

Like Lear and Cordelia, Ian and I discuss the 'who's in and who's out' nature of speedway book publishing. In a nutshell, I'm still stuck on the sidelines, while Ian has enjoyed some good sales and critical success but, as a fierce competitor, would always judge himself by more exalted standards. As a plain speaker, he also thinks some of the sales figures that I've heard, often apparently authoritatively, for recent rival publications is "b*******". He hopes that my signing goes well, though he has personal reservations as to whether the Belle Vue crowd are the biggest book purchasers in sharp contrast to their number, fervour and history.

Colin Meredith is also in the small speedway office that has been relocated since my last visit. He is an admired trackman whose curatorial skills have done so much recently to improve the reputation and standard of the racing circuit here, after investment in drains and materials by club owner Tony Mole. Despite the threat of rain, he's confident that the significantly improved drainage will allow the meeting to take place.

After I've hung about for a while, the older blokes on the pit gate tell me that John Jones, the Belle Vue track shop franchise holder, has just arrived in his van. Hopefully, the deserted main grandstand building might now be unlocked so that I can unload my boxes of books and set up my display table. For a high commission rate, John has kindly consented, albeit reluctantly, to give me special permission to display my books and sign them on a one-off basis. Demand to do this at Belle Vue is always likely to be high, given the importance and reputation of the club. When I arrive in the bar area where John is clearing his usual space for his track shop tables, he either has poor eyesight that causes him to contort his face or it's a look of withering contempt. We have a brief conversation in the bar.

Me: Hello John, where shall I go?

John: Freak off back to Eastbourne, you freaking prick.

Me: Er, you knew I was coming.

John: I have to put up with freaking pricks all the time, I'm a freaking professional and I'm freaking sick of freaking pricks like you.

Me: But where should I go, so I can keep out of your way?

John: You freaking better, over there by the door (waves his hand in direction of exit from bar to grandstand terraces), freaking do whatever you have to freaking do? What do you freaking do anyway?

Me: When I'm not here, ironically I'm a book publicist.

John: Well freak off back to that. I'm a freaking professional seller of merchandise, who's freaking mug enough to freaking pay rent to freaking sell my freaking stuff here, who's freaking constantly bothered by freaking pricks like you who have freaking big freaking ideas about selling on my pitch without freaking paying for it like I do.

Me: I'll pay you the commission we agreed.

John: Freaking do whatever you have to do.

I beat a retreat back to the pits to collect my car. I bump back into Ian and Colin again by the tractor. Ian says, "I get on well with John though he can be a little bit difficult. Imagine how he would have reacted if I hadn't suggested that you ask his permission first? At least he hasn't said you can't display your book." They both suggest that I position myself by the turnstiles, since it would be the best location to catch people since many fans choose to go upstairs to watch rather than wander through the bar to the grandstand. Ian informs me that as part of Jason Crump's contract - previously agreed with John Perrin – he has the right to exclusively sell his own branded merchandise at the Belle Vue track. "I don't have a problem with that and Jason gives all the profits he makes to a children's charity so it's in a good cause and it's in his contract. When John found out he went ballistic and demanded we throw Crumpie out; Crumpie wasn't happy either as it was in his contract – it was like World War III down there. John also understandably wasn't happy when Chris Morton signed his book here either – without permission or commission, but he is 'Mr Belle Vue' so he had to put up with it. I've always got on well with John, so you must speak as you find and he does rent the pitch so you can understand it and I did warn you to ask. Just let it go over your head is the best way."

Colin says, "I'd chin anyone who spoke to me like that".

I return to the bar and broach the subject of moving my pitch to the apparently prime position by the turnstiles with John.

Me: Ian says by the programmer seller might be a better place for me to stand.

John: Did he?

Me: Yes.

John: Well you freaking can't.

Me: Why?

John: I'm freaking telling you.

Me: Why?

John: 'Cause of freaking health and freaking safety.

Me: How come the programmer seller can stand there?

John: Freak knows.

Me: Are you in charge of health and safety here?

John: No.

Me: Well I'll wait until they tell me to move then.

John (waves at his space in the bar): Is it freaking alright if I freaking go here then?

Me: I'm not telling you where to go.

John: You freaking seem to think you freaking own the place.

Charming Lady Wife: Let's not even freaking bother to freaking unload, freaking pricks

John: I'm a freaking professional, I pay freaking thousands a year for freaking here, I'm not a freaking prick though people treat me like I freaking am. You stand there and every freaking prick will want to freaking stand there, they'll all get freaking big freaking ideas and it'll attract more freaking pricks like you. (walks towards van) I'm a freaking professional, a freaking seller of freaking merchandise and you're a freaking prick.

Charming Lady wife (disembodied voice from inside the van): Let's just not freaking bother, let's go and leave the freaking prick to it.

Me: I'm just trying to display my books, for which you gave me permission last week when I consulted you and we agreed your commission.

John: Freak off and stay out of my way, do whatever you freaking have to freaking do and don't freaking bother me (walks off with box back into the building) you freaking prick.

I wait in my car until the milk of human kindness has possibly started to flow and they have finished unloading. I then, totally predictably, find that the emergency exit doors that they'd been happy to leave unlocked and ajar throughout the lengthy time it took them to unload have now been locked shut to bar this access to the building. Smiling to myself, I drive my car back to the pits and so now I get some additional exercise as I have to walk the length of the home straight to take my boxes to the turnstiles area, where I have permission to do whatever I freaking want to do. I think I might go forth and multiply.

In sharp contrast to John 'I'm a freaking professional you freaking prick' Jones and his charmingly abrasive lady wife, everyone else I encounter at Belle Vue apparently doesn't have a chip on their shoulder and isn't foul-mouthed, abusive, resentful or paranoid. They have all obviously been properly brought up by their parents to treat others in the manner that they'd expect to be treated themselves. Out by the still-closed turnstiles, the talk among the security staff centres on worries that the new owners of the GRA are rumoured to be keen to get rid of all staff aged over 65 before they are subject to the age discrimination legislation that enters the UK statute book later in 2006. Anyhow, that is what the staff understands to be their aim. Many of the people employed here are senior citizens with considerable service and, although they only work part-time, their work as a security man or parking attendant at greyhound and speedway meetings is something that they really value and enjoy. It's both work and provides welcome frequent socialisation with other people – welcome at any age but particularly in older age. Judged by the hours I spend with them, they're very conscientious, naturally people-friendly and can't do enough to help others with directions, banter and assistance. Just the kind of conscientious and friendly employees that any company would ideally want to employ if their business requires that they regularly have to deal with the public and value good customer relations.

My book doesn't prove popular so instead I content myself with trying to give out leaflets that advertise it. Most people are happy to take one though some react as though I've made an improper suggestion and one man mysteriously says as he refuse to take one, "no thank you, I don't have a website". I overhear another lady say to the man she's with, "that's the chappie whose book you're reading". In the end I only sell one copy of the book to a man who loves the book but has left his copy in Tenerife. He's enjoying it so much that he can't wait to be reunited with it. It's strange to hear that one of the few copies that I've sold has already travelled so far! Even on an evening threatened with dark rain clouds, the Aces attract a large number of people through the turnstiles. Lynn Wright, James's mum, busily helps out with ferrying the cash from the turnstiles to locations unknown and Jayne Moss, Buxton co-promoter and Aces fan, works very energetically all evening, despite being noticeably heavy with child.

The meeting itself starts promptly and is almost straightaway under the threat of abandonment due to the light drizzle. This always has an impact on rider safety, not so much for the detrimental impact on the track conditions but because of how it affects the riders' vision. Nonetheless, the referee Dave Dowling runs the heats quickly. The Belle Vue riders cope better with the drizzle, though they don't really establish a commanding lead until Heat 9 (sponsored by the renowned jokers and notable Aces fans the "Mancunian Mexicans"), a race that is notable for a fine victory on the line for James Wright over Nicki Pedersen (as he slows too early to coast to victory) after a determined last gasp dash up the inside. It's a great scalp for James, who appears understandably delighted with his victory. I stand throughout the later heats with Richard Frost, whom I thank for his kind words in the programme, and John Turner who writes the reports each week for the *Speedway Star*. I learn a lot by just listening to the chitter-chatter of their conversation between races. Earlier, after Kenneth Bjerre has been beaten by Eastbourne's Joel Parsons, Richard remarks with chagrin, "[the result of that race] with Bjerre finishing last behind someone he should beat every time and would in Poland or Sweden, is precisely why we won't win the Elite League this year."

While we wait for the next race, a car owner is summoned to his car over the tannoy. Apparently feral youths from the nearby estates regularly choose to break into cars parked outside the impressive security fence that surrounds the stadium car park (but that requires payment to enter). Since, as I've noted before, speedway provides the ideal distraction for car thieves – we're all otherwise occupied for 90 minutes with our concentration directed elsewhere as well as the additional advantage that the noise of the bikes provides suitable camouflage.

David Norris has had his sense of humour stolen if his reaction at the end of Heat 11 is anything to gauge things by. Though he finished second (on a tactical ride), he pointedly stops by the start/finish line and picks up the red and black flags, ostentatiously waves them at the referee up in his box and then melodramatically throws them to the floor. This is probably tragedy, comedy, sour grapes or farce depending on your point of view. The meeting ends after the next race without the formality of a track inspection so that, though abridged, the result can still stand.

The crowd flood out through the exits and I wander round to the stand of the club's freaking professional John Jones. After he's finished serving his customer in a butter wouldn't melt in his mouth kind of way, the affected bonhomie immediately fades as he turns to me. I tell him of the limited success of my evening – one copy sold – and proffer his agreed albeit meagre commission. "It don't matter," he barks, though his eyes betray his words. Strangely, for a "freaking professional", he fails to ask about stocking my book. If you judge his merchandise solely by the quality of the badges on sale on his stall, he prefers to stock the modern shoddy-quality identikit versions rather than source the high quality ones that embodied craftsmanship, attention to detail and tradition that previously used to be available at track shops everywhere. Hardly surprising, when I think about it afterwards in the car.

I leave after I thank Ian Thomas and outside his office I bump into the always avuncular and cheerful Trevor Geer, Eastbourne co-team manager who's here tonight without Jon Cook because of his knee operation. "Oh hello, how are you? I've read some of the book [borrowed from his son Chris]. It's much better than the usual boring speedway book full of stats or races from long ago – really good, well done". It's genuine people like Trevor, throughout all of speedway really, that washes away the lingering taste that John "I.A.F.P.Y.P" Jones leaves.[1]

The M6 was so awful last week, against all my principles and stupidly in the light of my earnings, I decide to try the toll road that is the Midlands Expressway. Wow – what a great experience. I say this to the tollbooth man along with "it's my first time". He says, in careworn fashion, "yeah, it can be alright at this time of night but in the rush hour it's a different story". An honest reaction, if an off-putting one, which definitely isn't on any pre-prepared script. At 1 a.m. the mystery of the universe in the form of 'why there are such active and noisy ornamental fountains outside the service station building at Junction 8 of the M40 during a drought in Southern England?' still remains unsolved. Creating an improved ambience must be an essential business use after all.

19th June 2006 Belle Vue v Eastbourne (Elite League B) 44-30 (abandoned after 12 heats)

....

[1] in all fairness John rightly protects the pitch that he hires each week throughout the season from unnecessary competition. It's also refreshingly honest of him to make absolutely no attempt to dress up or disguise his contempt since I know exactly where I stand with him. Nowhere. I much prefer the honesty of this approach rather than two-facedness.

Unofficial 'Keep Britain Tidy' campaign starts

The lure of the Buxton versus Stoke local derby in the Conference League led me to schedule a few days in the North-West so that I could take in a football game and a trip to Belle Vue with my good friend Stefan Usansky. He used to go to Hyde Road in the glory days and his speedway re-education as a returnee to the sport in the twenty-first century has previously taken him to speedway meetings at Arlington and Wimborne Road. Every time I visit Manchester it appears rain is compulsory and, though the journey to Buxton speedway is beautiful, only blind optimism made it likely that the meeting would be on after a journey there in continuous rain. When we arrived at a windswept track there were still a substantial number of volunteers present, though they were sensibly sheltering in the sea container in the pits that serves as the lair and tearoom for the track staff. While in the referee's box, a damp but cheery Jayne Moss told us that they had hoped to run the meeting but the heavy rain that swept in during the morning (when she was at football with her son Josh) had reluctantly forced her husband Richard's decision to postpone, despite the fact that pretty well everything was already prepared for the meeting. A chirpy John Rich and 'Mushy Pea' (ICA Crook) were just about to depart the scene too having recently unloaded the car of speedway merchandise into the trackshop, only then to reload it again. The slightly desolate walk from the car park to the stadium and back in cold winds and lashing rain wasn't exactly ideal conditions for Stefan, with a hacking cough to indicate that his remission from lung cancer perhaps wasn't all that it was claimed. After the long drive back we dined early evening in a Greek restaurant in Sale where, towards the end of the meal (after dark), the waiter cheerfully told us, "You wouldn't believe it round here on a Friday and Saturday night!" Apparently the place where we had chosen to eat was located in an area known as a knife crime hotspot far worse than places you'd automatically think would fall victim to this lawless behaviour. Even though it was a Sunday night, it's never good to accidentally find yourself after nightfall in an area notorious for unprovoked knife1 attacks. Perhaps the restaurant management could feature this as a unique selling point in their future adverts?

The next day saw the weather gods look kindly on the Belle Vue fixture with Swindon and the sky is almost cloudless. Later we'll all be treated to a lovely crimson and blue sky that supposedly indicates that the shepherds in this area will be delighted. A difficult campaign for Belle Vue speedway from the outset of the season has supposedly been reflected in the crowd numbers but, whatever the truth or otherwise in these rumours, it's the kind of foregone conclusion of a meeting that any promoter would dread and surely would (particularly during a season like the 2007 one) only attract the hard core of die-hard Aces fans along to watch.

Earlier in the season, the 'A' fixture had seen Belle Vue lose 38-54 though tonight the often injury-ravaged Aces are arguably stronger since they have Simon Stead rather than a guest replacement, plus they have notionally been improved by the mid-season addition of Antonio Lindback in their side. Stead was injured (for the first time in an injury plagued 2007 season) on my last visit here for the meeting versus Eastbourne on a bitterly cold night when Nicki Pedersen reinforced his hate figure status among some sections (well, the Manchester Mexicans plus some other randomly aggrieved parties) of the Kirkmanshulme Lane crowd. Stefan had come along that night too and taken quiet satisfaction in the Aces 50-43 victory, while being the only person to wear a Manchester United bobble hat (minus the bobble) in the pits. That night the famous guitarist from the heyday of The Smiths – Johnny Marr – had attended as a guest of Bob Brimson the Eastbourne co-promoter with extensive music industry connections. Though we stood next to him, I regret not taking the opportunity for a brief word. Stef also noticed Johnny but only really because of his long hair rather than any real idea of who he was. Now that we're back inside the stadium via the pits gate, as guests of the Belle Vue promotion, it's clear that this whole area has been further remodelled in the five months since April 2nd. The most notable additions to the pits area aren't any of the permanent changes but the green awninged sideless tent erected in a prominent position parallel with the first bend under which to display a sparkling array of vintage speedway bikes. Like shoes on an army parade, everything about these machines glistens (including the huge pride of their owners), despite the lack of sunlight. Always curious about his environment and keen to meet people, Stef soon has the owners explain to him at great length the technical and maintenance aspects of their respective pride and joys. The copious technical detail soon loses me. The bikes do look lovely and with the metalwork burnished so brightly, these JAP bikes look magnificent. Stef marvels at the display of these machines since they immediately take him back to his youth and allow them all to reminisce about the privilege of the experiences they regularly had on race nights at Hyde Road.

They're all friendly men who're quickly mutually enthralled, though I have to drag Stef back from down memory lane for the short walk towards the main grandstand where I've been invited by Gordon Pairman on behalf of the Directors of Belle Vue speedway to display my books. I have their permission to base myself wherever I like to sell and display them, so again I choose to locate myself at the open plan area that's located just inside the turnstile entrance. From here all Belle Vue fans who enter the stadium have to pass either Stefan or myself. Those fans on their way upstairs to watch through the giant windows of the home straight grandstand, encounter Stefan handing out a leaflet cum postcard about my book. Since the upstairs has been developed to appease the demands of greyhound punters and liberate them from their money in some comfort, you definitely get a panoramic view of the track and a good selection of tables to sit at. That said, in my opinion, speedway isn't a sport to watch indoors, never mind behind glass, unless you have no choice in the matter. The alternative route for the fans is to stream past my small display table of books by the double doors that lead through to the rather dingy bar area that, after yet more fire doors, eventually leads out into the open air. From there, the choices are to remain on the concrete stepped terraces of the home straight under the lee of the roof or head off to take your chance exposed to the elements and stand on the fourth, third or second bends.

Completely thoughtlessly, I've already made a subsequently significant error of courtesy. I'd already been given express permission to display my books by Gordon Pairman (one of the Belle Vue promoters) but forgot to alert the trackshop owner of my intentions prior to my visit. Fortunately, I had previously agreed some comparatively usurious terms of trade for book sales on these premises with said owner of the speedway trackshop concession at Kirkmanshulme Lane, Mr John Jones. He's a territorial man and, like so many other people who've made his acquaintance, we've not exactly been bosom buddies – indeed he studiously ignored me at Cardiff and Newport, despite my attempts to be cordial – since our last encounter here in 2006. Nonetheless, common courtesy cuts both ways and dictates that I should have had enough professionalism to apprise him of my visit before I began to hand out my leaflets to the incoming fans.

Giving the lie to claims on reduced numbers through the turnstiles, an endless stream of Aces fans wend their way past us. Despite his 42 years in the book trade (32 in publishing sales and a decade in bookselling), Stef had never had the often soul-destroying experience of trying to pass on a leaflet to passing strangers who are often insulted, disquieted or suspicious of receiving such 'gifts'. I put this down to the fact that when you're handed something in the street you almost definitely never use the service or product advertised and view any product claims made with the utmost suspicion. Though my leaflet is the exception that disproves the rule, in this context we're really as welcome as a vegan in a crowded late-night kebab shop. Repeatedly saying the same phrase ("would you like a leaflet?") soon dries the mouth and saps your energy, though Stef approached it with his usual friendliness, vim and vigour. In fact, he started his own one-man campaign to test and record the limits of civility on a Monday night at Kirky Lane by being even more ultra-gracious than usual. This increased unctuousness soon has him amass (and record) a much larger number of "thank yous" from passing fans than I manage in the same time period. As the new boy to the discipline of smiling like a synchronised swimmer at a speedway meeting (often in the face of deliberate or unconscious abruptness), his enthusiasm levels are high but his energy levels are low. Though we soon swap places so he can hand out the leaflets sitting down by the book table, nonetheless, his volume of "thank yous" continues to increase, thereby indicating that it's his warmth and showmanship that elicit the response not the position of the pitch. Stef believes that people in the North are significantly friendlier than in the South and feels that this vindicates his feeling that Manchester people confirm this geographical divide. Allied to this affability is his innate (and almost blood-conscious) salesmanship that soon has book sales increase exponentially. Well, technically sales increased by infinity as I'd achieved none and he soon had sold two as well as nearly making me almost want to buy one as a result of the earnest, sincere and loving way he spoke about them. It's a rare skill and on my extensive travels only Alf Weedon and Johnny Barber have exhibited this potent combination of enthusiasm, plausible genuineness and killer sales instinct.

We barely make it round to the pits to stand in the new viewing area for visitors and guests ("you can see everything but the track" Jonathan Bethell notes standing by me – something forgotten in the pits whenever the decision of the sight-challenged referee perched high in the grandstand is queried) before Leigh Adams fires off from the start gate and disappears into the distance, comfortably ahead of Simon Stead and James Wright. Though the race is drawn there was such a huge distance between the Aces and the Robins captain at the finish that this really doesn't bode well for the remainder of the meeting. As if to emphasise the gulf between the teams, Andrew Moore wins the next race from the gate. He shows considerable delight when he crosses the line, though his victory lap of celebration only gets as far as the first bend before he falls (conveniently) in front of the pits gate to loud, ironic cheers from the Belle Vue fans on the terraces. The next three races all result in heat advantages for the Robins and, consequently, Simon Stead appears out in the sixth heat on a tactical ride. It's an inspired choice by joint team managers Eric Boocock and Chris Morton since not only does Stead win but James Wright follows up his rear for an 8-1. This brings the scores back to a much more manageable 18-21 and the delighted announcer informs the assembled faithful, "That's more like it!" And it briefly is until Charlie Gjedde and Lee Richardson combine in the next race with an immediate 5-1 reply for the Robins that silences the crowd except for a small section of (so-called) Aces fans on the grandstand terraces, who loudly barrack Antonio Lindback and doubt his parentage because of his inopportune engine failure.

With the interval approaching, Stef and I rush from the comfort and safety of the pits back towards the grandstand where I intend to resume trying to sell my books to the Aces faithful. At the last World Cup the Japanese fans were a real hit with the stadium owners after they stayed behind for an hour after the game to clean their section of the stand. They always left it tidier than they found it. Increasingly nowadays people throw rubbish and litter wherever the fancy takes them. It's one of those tiny but extremely visible signs of selfishness that seems to characterise the use of public spaces everywhere you look in Britain. As previously explained, whenever I travel to speedway tracks round the country I try to entice people to think about buying the books I've got on display by handing them a leaflet. Some people are very reluctant to take it, some immediately tear it into shreds and others actually say "thank you". Handing them out at the home of Belle Vue speedway I reached 43 "thank yous" and so narrowly lost to my friend Stefan who'd got to 48 when he stopped counting far earlier than I did. Once the speedway bug for statistics has bitten it's hard to shake!

Everywhere I go, after the meeting, I try to find as many of these discarded leaflets as I can and place them in the bin provided or take them home again to throw away. I do this partly so as not to irk my hosts or the stadium owners with my additional litter but also, more selfishly, I'm vainly trying to preserve some residual cache for my books by attempting to make them look valued. Belle Vue trackshop merchant, John Jones obviously takes a territorial pride in his workplace and, unbeknownst to me, during the early heats of the meeting he'd kindly taken it upon himself to conscientiously pick up all the dropped leaflets he could find scattered around the bar area and meticulously shredded them for recycling. I admire any example of environmentalism but didn't expect to find such a committed and avid eco-warrior in the speedway merchandise community. Sadly I didn't know that I should thank him for this service when I bumped into him, just before the interval of the Elite B fixture against then league leaders Swindon. I said, "Ah, John, how are you?" They say cleanliness is next to godliness and the extremely territorial Mr. Jones clearly doesn't have much truck with litterbugs like me promoting their books on his chosen patch. With admirable passion for the environment, he replied angrily.

"You've got a farking cheek you Farking **** showing your face here. You can fark off! Don't you farking call me a 'Freaking Professional' who the fark do you think you are, you ****. You're getting a farking solicitor's letter you ****. I was hiring two farking blokes to sort you out farking properly for next week [the visit of Eastbourne on September 10th]. I didn't farking expect you this week. I hope you're farking coming 'cause they're farking booked! I've got a farking bag of confetti for you [calls to wife 'where's the bag for the ****? His farking confetti!'] 'There you go you farking ****! There's your farking confetti [hands over the plastic bag of ripped up leaflets he'd kindly picked up] You've got a farking cheek. Fark **** – your solicitor's letter is on its way. Don't you farking 'freaking professional' me. Farking writing that – think you're so farking clever. I'm demanding a farking apology from Philip Rising[2] You **** and, if not, you're farking for it, you're dead, the farking solicitor's letter is on its way and I want every farking penny commission from tonight. Every farking penny you ****! Showing your farking face. If you print a farking word, you're dead! Fark off you ****!"

---

[2] I subsequently learn that John Jones had written a letter to the editor of the *Speedway Star* objecting to a brief mention of his behaviour outlined in my book in an article written by Peter Oakes that appeared in the magazine. It's probably always best to avoid unnecessary legal action but quite why an apology was required for alluding to his original poor behaviour written in my book remains a complete mystery to me.

Postscript: This conversation with John Jones, trackshop man at Belle Vue speedway, was held at 8.20 p.m. on September 3rd 2007. This conversation comes from my contemporaneous (shakily) hand written notes composed immediately afterwards in the grandstand bar though I didn't really take in the panoramic view. Throughout his tirade, Mr Jones stood extremely close to fulminate and threateningly jabbed a finger at my face repeatedly – he appeared to struggle to restrain himself from hitting me. I said nothing at all in reply, though my guest, Stefan Usansky witnessed the whole event and frequently interjected with "what disgusting language" a number of times, but to no avail. Afterwards Stefan said incredulously, "I've never come across anyone like that in my life!" More importantly, he couldn't believe that such an ostensibly family-oriented sport as speedway could harbour such a repugnant individual in any position of responsibility, let alone in charge of the trackshop of the club he's followed since his youth!

Quite what you do after such threats isn't easy to decide when you're shaken by the ferocity of the conversation itself. I subsequently learnt that the SCB official in charge of a meeting has the powers to exclude anyone they choose from the stadium whom they deem to be behaving detrimentally towards the safe running of the meeting. These powers apply to anywhere within the stadium so this includes the fans just as much as the riders, officials and mechanics. The natural inclination in the face of threatening behaviour that you take seriously – which I did – is to report it to the police. We all know that policemen are not required at speedway meetings and this remains a genuine source of pride to us all within the speedway community. Equally going to the police station afterwards in a city you don't come from is bound to complicate things and, anyway, it really doesn't seem sensible to run the good name of the club and speedway through the mud because of the reprehensible attitude of one peculiar individual. On top of that everyone at the club has been unfailingly friendly. When I get back to the pits I explain what has happened to the head of security who tells me that John Jones is all hot air and should be ignored. He insists that I should attend the next meeting at Kirkmanshulme Lane when Eastbourne are due to visit and I'd come along as part of my Writer in Residence duties. This is easy for him to blithely say. I'm reluctant to tempt providence or John Jones's temper but he reassures with "don't worry if he starts anything some of mine are itching for the excuse to sort someone out!" Without wishing to interrupt their enjoyment of the meeting, I also briefly explained the conversation and threats to Gordon Pairman and David Gordon (whom I met for the first time). They were shocked and apologetic on behalf of the club but pointed out that when they completed their takeover at the club many other matters directly relating to the actual functioning of the speedway club took their immediate priority and attention. The relationship with John Jones and the fact that he was in charge of the speedway franchise at the club wasn't their choice but an inheritance from the previous Tony Mole regime at Belle Vue. Also, technically, Jones is really a franchisee at the stadium on speedway race nights who rents his pitch from the stadium owners the GRA. So, ultimately, responsibility for his supervision and behaviour falls under their jurisdiction. Not that the Belle Vue promotion were washing their hands of responsibility and they assured me that they would be having strong words with John Jones at the earliest opportunity to highlight their displeasure and concern as well as identifying to him what they consider to be the professional standards of behaviour they expect from anyone concerned with Belle Vue speedway club.[3] I must say that EVERYONE I met throughout my night as a guest of Belle Vue speedway (with their full permission to attend and sell my books as well as describe this incident in my book) were charming, friendly and affable or couldn't have been more helpful and supportive.

Though I watched the races and noted down the scores, the remainder of the meeting passed in blur as I sipped a hot strong cup of tea in the pits. It was Swindon's second away Elite League win at Kirkmanshulme Lane in 2007 and the final score at 35-58 was one point more than that achieved in the 'A' fixture. It was a record-breaking night for all the wrong reasons since this 10th home league defeat of the season set a new (unwanted) Aces record. In the 20 years the club have spent at Kirkmanshulme Lane, Swindon became the first visiting side to track three unbeaten riders during a meeting and it was the second heaviest loss ever at the track (after the 32-58 defeat by Poole in 2001). For reasons of tiredness, my friend Stefan wanted to leave the stadium without hanging around to try to sell more books by the stadium exit doors. My stubborn streak dictated that having come all this way I would persevere and I was rewarded with an additional sale and a charming conversation with the security people who, like so many others involved in the sport, had their own stories to tell about John Jones's irascibility that don't reflect well on him as an individual.

3rd September 2007 Belle Vue v Swindon (Elite League B) 35-58

[3] Afterwards Gordon Pairman wrote to me copying Chris Morton and David Gordon to say, "can I apologise for that man's appalling behaviour, please? I spoke to him after we spoke – actually it was closer to me shouting at him – and David, Chris and I discussed the incident at our board meeting on Tuesday. Although it is true that he is not an employee of Belle Vue, simply a franchise holder, we take our responsibilities seriously, and his attitude is simply unacceptable. I will do my utmost to ensure that your next visit is not marred in the same way."

Chapter Two – Eastbourne

....

I'm strangely nervous as I arrive for my first proper speedway meeting as the Eagles new Writer in Residence. Though all such thoughts are soon put aside when on the journey from the car park to the pits I meet one glamorous woman after another in quick succession in the form of Debbie Taylor, Anne-Mette, Louise Brimson and Jane Wooler. Louise has brought four month Lowell along for his first ever meeting and he attracts admirers like a magnet. One of these is Nicki Pedersen who pops over to tell his interested partner Anne-Mette "only borrow not making!" I'm always impressed by anyone who can display a sense of humour in a foreign language.

The pits are thronged with fans along with the staff, riders and mechanics of both teams. The Eagles track staff all appear in a 'Men in Black' look since most are smartly dressed in their new team anoraks. They'll all get a thorough test tonight since there is a perishing cold wind blowing through the stadium that feels like it accurately presages the weather forecast of possible snow ahead in the next few days. However, this is speedway and the riders appear impervious to the biting cold dressed in their kevlars, though some of them make a concession to the elements with beanie hats and coats. We breed the Clerk of the Course tough here as Malcolm Cole conspicuously wears his anorak open and unzipped all night and thereby shows off his collared shirt, tie and jacket that I gather SCB regulations insist upon. I imagine he only finally does it up when it gets really cold.

Poole have gone for the 'strong top two' philosophy this year in their team building plans and the addition of Jason Crump to their roster of riders further adds to the considerable lustre and quality reputation that they already enjoy as a club. Jason's father Phil is also in the pits and his son strides confidently about the place. Since I'm so close I notice for the first time how broad shouldered he is but, then again, maybe he always was or perhaps this is a result of his close season fitness campaign. He's expected to make a big impact on the track – in the 2006 season he was a class apart everywhere he rode – but it's off the track that his real commercial impact is felt. The always affable and considerate Poole Press Officer, Gordie Day, admires the new look Eagles programme but notes "ours is very different as it's almost completely full of adverts – people may mock but companies everywhere always want to be linked with success and the news that we have Jason has had the phone ringing constantly". Also in attendance is Poole co-promoter and tonsorial expert, Matt Ford, who is almost unrecognisable since he presently sports David Cameron's nut-brown hair colour rather than his usual distinctive blonde highlights. Also on the Poole side of the pits in their enclosure that overlooks the second bend is Arlington legend Gordon Kennett who looks on intently throughout and presently remains the Eagles all time highest points scorer with a total of 5339. In a handy table of past and present riders who've worn the Eagles colours prepared by Sid Shine that appears in the programme, we can see that this total will shortly be overhauled by Floppy. It's a list that contains an impressive six Kennetts and three Dugards!

The changes that have swept Arlington in the close season even extends to the toilets by the first bend where an OAP tells Isle of Wight co-promoter and SCB committee member Dave Pavitt, "well it smells a lot fresher in here this year". Without any need to sniff the air to confirm the veracity of this observation, the always-witty Mr Pavitt responds "yeh, but I still wouldn't like to eat my sandwiches in here but I know what you mean."

A large crowd continues to flood through the turnstiles and past the programme stall where Bob Brimson, his brother Greg and wife Louise hand out free air horns emblazoned with the new Eagles logo to interested children. The track shop has the commercial good sense to be awash with merchandise badged with this new extremely distinctive logo and a casual glance round the terraces soon confirms that some fans already wear their 2007 season anoraks with pride. It's so cold I buy an Eagles hat before I retreat to the warmth of the announcers box from which the dulcet tones of the hard-working eponymous Bryn Williams already rings out, "Dave Croucher and Dave Pavitt are both here tonight and I'm sure that they'll be in the bar later!" Bryn shows me his leg and what I mistake for sensible long johns turns out to be a knee length surgical bandage for his sceptic corn, which he attempts to cure with a quick cigarette in the windy doorway of the box. He's appalled to learn that smoking will be banned throughout Arlington Stadium from 1 July "what everywhere? Even outside? But I thought Brimson was a smoker too?"

I check in where I usually stand (board 49 this year) with Eagles fanatics, the Hazelden family, to find out their considered opinions for the season ahead. There's strong disagreement among them. Mark insists, "we'll be in the play offs. It's the strongest team we've had down here for two or three years and we're 16-1 to win the league, which is worth a bet. This team reminds me of some of our underestimated great sides plus we've a promoter that gives a monkeys and a team manager who cares." His father John isn't so easily convinced "I'll give it 10 heats before I can tell you who should go" before he prematurely names the likely candidates. Meanwhile his wife Judy is delighted by the return of Stefan Andersson, "he's the man – Stef is bloody good for us and he'd ride through fire for Eastbourne!"

It appears smokers skulk everywhere at Arlington, so it's no surprise that I spot tonight's SCB official Chris Gay deep in conversation and mid fag sheltered in the lee of the St John Ambulance hut. Back in the pits the "two Daves" from the Isle of Wight look forward to the season ahead and have come along to keep a close eye on their gifted young Australian rider Jason Doyle ("Doyley"). As is traditional at the first team meeting of the season, Dave Croucher will present the probably completely mystified Islander's riders with a 5p coin each along with a note that says "CMAX CMAX CMAX" This is all part of his lesson in preparation for the riders (the CMAX in question is Max who runs the spares van on the Island) for their road trips ahead, "they should always travel with their own spares – inner tubes, clutch cables and the like - cos legally the tracks only have to provide tyres and fuel. In the Elite League that's fine cos someone always has something but in the PL it's more make do and mend. King's Lynn, Rye House and Redcar are fine but if you don't prepare and bring spares, it'll freak up your road trip when things go wrong". The model professional they always cite as the pre-eminent example of this forewarned is forearmed approach is former Islanders rider Craig Boyce ("Boycie") "though even Boycie quietly said to me 'you know I don't take an inner tube'". As we talk the track staff scatter large bags of sawdust onto the first bend and Bob Dugard circles behind them with his tractor. Dave Pavitt is mystified, "what's he doing putting freaking sawdust down for then? I thought it looked perfect to me – he probably just wants to look busy".

The racing gets underway in stop-start fashion with a protracted first heat. In the first attempt to run the race, the Poole riders appear to move as the tapes rise without penalty before the meetings descends into the first controversy of the night when Edward Kennett comes heavily under David Norris on the second bend (of the second lap) to throw him unceremoniously from his bike. This happens right by my position but takes place in what is effectively a blind spot for the referee and, as Bob Brimson notes, "they all know exactly where it is". Chris Gay's view diagonally across the circuit from the box will inevitably provide a radically different perspective than that of those close by. Consequently, it's no surprise that Norris is deemed at fault and excluded. In the re-run Deano fails to make the gate but uses cunning and his local track knowledge to hug the white line to sneakily blast up the inside of Edward Kennett. Sadly he then falls on the second lap when completely unchallenged at the opposite end of the track to thereby force Edward to lay down his machine with great alacrity. This means that the first heat of the Brimson era ends in the worst possible fashion with an awarded 5-0 to the Pirates. Things don't look so clever in the next until Troy Batchelor gets out of shape and, what was a comfortably smooth exhibition of team riding, instantly descends into confusion when Doyley clatters into him. The exclusion for Troy leaves the scorecard already marked with so many crosses it has started to resemble a pools coupon.

The battle of the Pedersens has first blood to Nicki though Bjarne threatens his position throughout. The next winner is Poole's not-so-secret-weapon in the form of "veteran" Craig Boyce who appears to effortlessly continue his spectacular form of last season. Two heats later he repeats the treatment when he aggressively skittles past David Norris to record another comfortable victory. In between these races, there is another Australian victor – Jason Crump – who massacres Nicki Pedersen in the first bend with a show of exceptional speed that has the Dane trail behind before the onset of mechanical gremlins has him theatrically shake his head as he trails off further and further behind. If you can establish psychological mastery in a single race, then the first encounter of the season is as good a place as any to start from. The camaraderie and team spirit that is evident all around in the Eagles camp sparks even further into life when Davey Watt triumphs over Bjarne Pedersen in heat 7. This narrows the score to 20-21 but also signals a cue to rush to the fence for Floppy, Nicki and Trevor Geer, who wave congratulation, and by the safety barrier for Bob Brimson to thrust his arms aloft. Club physio, Jane Wooler, notes, "it's like a family here, no-one's on their own in this lot – if one person comes last we all come last and if one wins we all win!" Team spirit also courses strongly through the Pirates camp, if judged by the evidence provided by the sight of Jason Crump running half the length of the back straight to offer words of advice to a disconsolate Troy Batchelor as he wheels his bike back after an unfortunate engine failure while placed second in the eighth heat. It's a costly failure since it enables the Barker-Bridger partnership to record a 5-1 that takes the Eagles into their first lead of the season.

In the same way that an alcoholic is someone who drinks as much as you except that you don't like them, so it is with speedway riders who're described as 'hard' if they ride for your team but 'dirty' if they don't. A random straw poll before the meeting to identify the 'hard' riders in either team would have probably thrown up the names of Craig Boyce, Jason Crump and Nicki Pedersen, particularly the latter who is often the rider every opposition fan often loves to hate. One of the unspoken rules of the sport is that you should try to leave your opponent 'enough' room to race, though the problem often comes from the fact that the definition of 'enough' is always in the eye of the beholder. Whatever the exact calibration of such measurements, there's no doubt that Nicki has attracted more than his fair share of controversy (people still talk about the incident in the GPs with Greg Hancock) while Boycie is often remembered for the punch thrown at Tomas Gollob. Presciently in his programme notes on the away side (hence he doesn't offer any opinion on Nicki), Alex Raby says "Craig's reputation precedes him" before he trots out the well-worn description of "veteran" Boycie as like a "fine wine" before he then adds, "however, unlike a wine, he lacks a soft texture, preferring a hard and determined riding style which leaves a tang in your mouth". The incipient tension of the pits all night exacerbated by local rivalry bubbles instantly to the surface during heat 9 when Boycie appears to deliberately drive hard through the second bend in a manner that ensures that Nicki Pedersen has an enforced encounter with the air fence. Initial thoughts that they're a day late for some speedway style Comic Relief sponsored fundraiser is quickly dispelled by the sheer aggression and rancour of the ensuing fracas. My contemporaneous impression – and the incident happened right in front of my vantage point - is that this was a calculated manoeuvre by one rider placed ahead of another rider who was in a position to both control his racing line and in sufficient form not to have to bother with such an aggressive tactic. But then, that's the thrill and unpredictability of speedway. Needless to say Nicki wasn't enamoured with this tactic and remonstrated with the stricken Boycie in manner that caused Craig to leap to his feet and punch/lash out in an attempt to inflict his own Red Nose on the Danish rider. I understand that Nicki placed his own helmet close enough to Craig to inspect the safety certification kite mark but without actual contact in the form of either a head butt or a punch. However, the air fence blocked my view of this incident since it occurred below the level of the fence on the track surface. The view from the Poole side of the pit lane would also be similarly obscured so anyone who claims to have seen this alleged 'head butt' incident live must have x-ray eyes. However, whatever did happen would be clear to anyone located on the centre green or in the referee's box.

A thrown punch is signal for a brief but impressively attended melee to ensue that has the erstwhile protagonists separated from each other with some flailing determination by riders and staff from both teams. It's an intervention that staunches the flow of adrenalin and prevents further confrontation between Boyce and Pedersen but leaves the pits area in a tumultuous frenzy of raised voices, waved arms and people who dash hither and thither. Jason Crump pointedly intervenes as a 'peacemaker' with Nicki back inside the 'neutral' area of the pits and takes some moments to, I imagine, counsel calm just as a visible welt appears to grow on Nicki's cheek. Shortly afterwards and while the punctured air fence is repaired, Bob Dugard leaves his tractor to calm the situation and offer some words to the wise. The aftermath remains confused for some minutes and there's a cacophony of opinion, hearsay and rumour. I can only catch snippets of conversation and fail to identify who said "there's a lot of bad feeling cos we freaking hate each other" though I did hear

Malcolm Cole "my opinion is that I'd exclude him from the meeting – there was no need for that – I've never before asked the ref for such a thing"

Nicki "they say I punched him – they're making up stories over there with the biggest freaking liar in the whole world"

Dave Croucher "what happened? Oh. I've never been to any meeting yet without some trouble – though it's usually fairly minor"

Greg Brimson [affects accent] "Bob [Dugard] said, 'we'll see what happens'"

Bob Brimson "I think he definitely took him off"

Photographer Mick Hinves gleefully "I caught it all"

With contending voices all around him, Chris Gay adjudicates and enforces the maximum justice allowed for within the SCB rulebook this situation. A "provoked" Boycie is excluded from the race for unfair riding, fined the maximum £300 and reported to the SCB for further judgement (or an encounter with their fabled carpet). Rumours that Boycie works in an unofficial capacity for the Australian Tourist Board as a cultural attaché with responsibility for Aussie-Danish relations are dismissed as idle speculation and, after further air fence repairs, the meeting eventually continues.

After the enforced unofficial interval break brought on by the contretemps, the race is rerun and predictably enough Nicki easily wins the rerun. In the next, a fired up David Norris scythes across the first corner with some determination but fails to collect Bjarne Pedersen who appears wise enough to predict his intentions to control his speed and thereby astutely avoid any unnecessary bother. Floppy's race win has an exultant Bob Brimson yell at the sky and jump up onto the crash barrier. Bjarne continues to have good clairvoyancy skills or has turned into Brer Pedersen since in heat 12 he anticipates that his namesake Nicki will aggressively try to charge from inside him in an attempt to drive him to the fence. Again careful control of his throttle avoids this eventuality and enables him to almost immediately repay his compatriot this intended favour on the next bend. It's a well-executed almost chess-like manoeuvre that leaves Nicki out by the fence and comprehensively second, though he initially chases to recover lost ground in desultory manner before mechanical gremlins again afflict his speed levels.

Heat 13 in the 2007 season is no longer what it once was since the two best riders from each team no longer meet then. However, the revised configuration does force a re-appearance outside the Poole side of the pits by Craig Boyce who the Eagles crowd then very half-heartedly boo for around a nanosecond. As before every race at Arlington, all the riders line up together in the pit lane to await the signal to move. In a show of support for his teammate Floppy ostentatiously avoids any eye contact with Boycie – when it would have been easier to do otherwise – and emphasizes this point when he loops round the stationary bikes to chat with Jason Crump instead. An isolated Boycie then shoots off down towards the track entrance gate with a speed that wouldn't disgrace a ram raider but then has to wait patiently at the closed gate for the track grade to finish. In the initial attempt to run this race, Davey Watt flies from the start and is then subject to what looked like a 'professional foul' from Jason that is ruled as 'first bend bunching' by the referee. In the rerun, Jason flies imperiously from the tapes, though Boycie chooses to pootle about at the rear of the field out of harm's way.

Bob Brimson remains in a state of high anxiety and, after Cameron Woodward falls and Stefan injures his foot when he collides with him in Keystone Cops fashion, is seized with a sense of doom "we're going to freaking lose this!" In the rerun the wounded Stefan fights his way past Jason Doyle but can't catch a triumphant Troy Batchelor who punches the air delightedly.

With a slender one-point lead, Trevor Geer springs a surprise when he nominates Davey Watt to partner Nicki ("I didn't think David was making the starts and thought it should be Davey") against the strong Crump-Pedersen pairing in the final race of the night. Against the odds that practically any bookie or fan would have offered Jason Crump finishes last having been held there by a combative Davey Watt. Whatever has gone on before, it's a hugely creditable display capped off with a victory for Nicki that featured a determinedly aggressive ride on the first lap to vanquish his erstwhile Poole rivals. Joy is unalloyed among the riders and mechanics. Bob Brimson leaps in the air though he's out jumped and out celebrated by Nicki's exultant mechanics, the father and son team of Ray and Mark Blackwell, who dance wildly. After the victory parade, Ray notes as he disassembles one of the bikes "Nicki can never accept a visiting number one coming to his track and scoring a maximum. He made the big decision to change to another bike – it costs money to prepare any bike – though he'd rode the rest of the meeting on one machine, this switch paid off!" The local reporters who're keen for an interview with Nicki all have to wait while he patiently poses for numerous photos for parents with young children in garments branded with his name.

Matt Ford allegedly refuses to discuss the incident with Boycie with inquisitive local reporters until he's seen the video. Over at the track shop, the Brighton Argus ladies have provided a poster for the track shop window that reads, "Alan Boniface is a Grandad". Though there is great pride in the pits, the arrival of one-week-old Katie evidently provides greater joy for Alan. After the junior races have finished and the meeting declared closed, Bryn Williams signs off with a phrase that he blames on his teeth but that sounds suspiciously like someone named "Kimono Bob Brimson" has opened his promotional reign at Arlington with a keenly contested win.

17th March 2007 Eastbourne v Poole (Elite League) 46-43

Chapter Three – Newcastle

....

The wonderful city of Newcastle upon Tyne is a great place to visit and spend some time, particularly if you're keen on going out to enjoy yourself socially on an evening. They take a zealous approach to relaxation and there's an enviable choice of places to go. This is especially so in the centre of the city and the regenerated quayside area by the river Tyne, where the recent years of social and cultural renaissance are most spectacularly visible. On the Sunday early afternoon that I visit, the centre is strangely deserted and there is a subdued atmosphere about the place. This isn't caused by the heavily overcast skies but due to the city's main passion, focus and, almost, its religion because its beloved football club starts another campaign of Premiership football with a televised lunchtime encounter with Arsenal. Expectations are at their usual exaggerated Olympian levels based on faith and belief rather than the actual record of results in terms of trophies and championships of the last five decades. Pretty well everyone who doesn't have a ticket for the match chooses to watch on TV in one of the many bars or at home. On any normal day the cultural, commercial and social vibrancy of this city would immediately stand out to any visitor.

The home of the Newcastle Diamonds Speedway Club at Brough Park is located over two miles away from downtown in one of the area's most famous locales, known as Byker. What an appropriate name for the part of the city in which to run speedway events! Since I am a regular visitor to this part of the country, I make a point to take full advantage of the excellent metro transport system, a sort of under- and overground train-cum-tram, that stretches in all directions throughout the area and as far away as the airport or Sunderland, the other nearby city that is sadly forlorn and neglected in comparison to Newcastle. In the course of the train journey to Byker station it bursts out from its underground tunnel into daylight to bestow a wonderful elevated view across the buildings at the core of the city, one that almost competes with the spectacular vista when the metro crosses the bridge over the Tyne. Once on foot, the walk to Brough Park takes you past the swimming pool, some newish blocks of flats built in the current brutalist style of fashionable hotels or offices, before you discover the more traditional terraced houses of Grace Street which then lead to the stadium's impressive perimeter fencing.

On an overcast and cloudy afternoon, I arrive at the stadium to meet with George English, the cheery co-promoter of Newcastle Diamonds Speedway. A small group of volunteer staff has already arrived but they find themselves locked outside the fortified fencing, since they're unable to gain access through the padlocked main entrance. These are the responsibility of the landlords, William Hill, and these dedicated volunteers all have to wait patiently to get on with the tasks that George so values their help with every week. I wait with them as they struggle to get in, before I leave them to wait for William Hill to fulfil their responsibilities and double back on myself to enter Brough Park through the open pits gate entrance. The car park just inside the gate entrance is already crowded with riders and their, mostly white, vans. The Somerset Rebels team, this evening's opponents for the Newcastle Diamonds have arrived early since they're already in this part of the world. Tonight is the third leg of their 'Northern Tour'; a trip on which they have already suffered defeats on successive nights at Edinburgh and Berwick. Just inside the gate Peter Toogood, the promoter of Somerset and Chairman of the BSPA, pulls out his briefcase from the boot of his car, unfastens it and then puts his tie on to add the final touch to his smart attire of collared shirt and trousers. According to his stepdaughter and co-promoter Jo Lawson, it's a compulsory SCB regulation for officials to look smart and present themselves well on race day. Later she leaves to go to change out of her own casual travel clothes. Peter looks slightly distracted when I greet him but he hopes for a closer meeting than the previous evening at Berwick, especially since Somerset have a good chance of gaining the bonus point due to the 24-point advantage they obtained through a 58–34 home triumph against the Diamonds in June. I pass an armada of riders' vans that includes Paul Fry's transit, whose side door is open to reveal his wife in a deep sleep on the specially customised bed, while their children play contentedly in the front seat. As I head off to meet George English in his office I stroll through the pits area, which looks out across the track itself and the stadium grandstand, which is filled with riders and mechanics who busily prepare the bikes for tonight's racing.

The track itself, located inside the tarpaulin-covered greyhound track, undergoes some last-minute preparations supervised by the club's experienced track manager, Robbie Best. These attentions mostly involve watering of the surface using the aged fire engine that serves as the bowser at Newcastle. Robbie has the weekly problem to attempt to prepare an ideal racing surface. He works within some very restrictive conditions that necessarily result from the speedway club's status as the mere one-day-a-week tenant of William Hill, the company who own and run this greyhound stadium. Though Robbie has the dispensation to spend the odd hour here and there during the week, he basically only has access to the track on the day of the actual meeting. Therefore, every Sunday during the season he arrives at first light to do everything he can to ensure the track is the best that it can before the traditional start time of 5.30 p.m. George later pays tribute to his skills, "he's so dedicated and spends an awful lot of time here" and praises the work of the regular track staff volunteers. Often this work is of a remedial nature, since the intensive use and maintenance of the dog track on the other six days of the week regularly results in damage to the speedway track surface; particularly troublesome is the sand leeched by the water drainage trenches from the dog track onto the shale race surface. These tribulations and the severe time constraints they all work under are part and parcel of the difficulties the speedway staff face on a weekly basis.

George already waits for me in the Speedway Office, which is housed in a slightly dilapidated building that also has the home and away riders' changing rooms in it, and a small kitchen area where somebody's grandmother cheerily washes the dishes and prepares the tea. George welcomes me into his office, surely one of the few speedway offices in the country with a comfy sofa, and we quickly start to discuss his life in speedway and some of the history of the club. He first visited the speedway at the age of four, brought by his mother Joan and father George who'd been "fanatical all his life" about speedway since he first began to go in the 1940s. Joan English is the very sprightly lady you usually see at all of the Diamonds away meetings thoroughly absorbed in the racing, who often urges the Diamonds riders on in her broad Geordie accent while she displays levels of energy that would be enviable in a considerably younger person. At Brough Park Joan has many tasks and responsibilities on race night ("I'm general dogsbody"), often in the office or at the turnstiles, so she has to take her racing pleasures where she can, "I love going away, it's when I get to see all me races, as I don't get to see a whole match here anymore, just the odd race". Speedway prides itself as a sport with a family emphasis, which is something that appeals to Joan who enjoys the "family orientation and involvement" among the spectators, staff and riders. I first encountered Joan accidentally at a Newcastle away meeting in Workington and, once you've noticed her, she cuts a very distinctive figure at the tracks she visits and is always notable for her energy, commitment and keen support of the Diamonds. This close-knit social emphasis you get at speedway is illustrated by today's contest between the Diamonds and the Rebels, which matches mother and son of Joan/George English for Newcastle versus the father and stepdaughter combination of Peter/Jo for Somerset.

The day-to-day experience of speedway promotion at Newcastle has, however, over the last few years been quite a struggle financially and throughout its existence the club has had a chequered history that has involved intermittent closures. George notes, "I've been here all my life, it's in my blood" but as a track it's "an outpost or feels like an outpost", both geographically and in the sports imagination of the city itself.

George became a promoter when Newcastle joined the newly formed Premier League in 1997 and it won't be long before he overtakes Ian Thomas (1975–84) as the longest serving boss in the club's history. Every promoter at the club has made a virtue of Newcastle's limited finances, the club has had to discover and develop young riders, so is renowned for its rich tradition and a selection policy that uses mostly unproven "foreign riders" before they, hopefully, develop into successful exponents of the sport. Each era has attracted different nationalities to Newcastle, in "the 1960s it was the Aussies and lately it's been the Danes". The list of famous riders who've successfully worn the distinctive black-and-white team race bibs is a roll call of speedway's great and good. It includes: Ivan Mauger ("my favourite and idol; from the age of four I was lucky to watch him go all the way through the sport to winning six World Championships"), Ole Olsen, Anders Michanek ("not my favourite as he hardly ever turned up"), the Owen brothers (Tom and Joe) as well as more recently the Pedersens (the unrelated Bjarne and Nicki) plus the diminutive Kenneth Bjerre. Though these riders and the teams they rode in have provided lustre to the great history of the club, George nowadays describes himself as "very much a Premier League person, full stop" and it's at this level they have enjoyed some recent notable success. The last triumph for the club was when they won the Premier League Championship in 2001 followed up with, George is keen to assert, a repeat "moral victory" in 2002 where they won more meetings than the eventual champions Sheffield (with their "home-track advantage"). George stresses, "while we lost out on race points difference, I look on ourselves as the rightful winners".

It's a truism, but correct nonetheless, that supporters in all sports are much more attracted to success than failure, so it's hardly a surprise that crowds at Brough Park fell dramatically the previous year when the team endured a shocker of a season and found themselves rooted last in the league. While this season the league position is slightly healthier and performances are much improved, the low crowd numbers still reflect the recent legacy of last season's poor results. George is characteristically phlegmatic if not quite able to solely blame the Diamonds' own performances, "our crowds aren't good this season but then we're also being squeezed on the one side by the Elite League and TV coverage and on the other by some not true Conference level sides". Newcastle ran a team for three years at a Conference level to develop young talent and refused to use experienced riders ("old hands") because it went against the ethos and true spirit behind the inauguration of the league, never mind the cost implications of having to pay too much.

The Diamonds also remain saddled with a very high rent for the use of the stadium and its facilities. Especially as it now uses only a small proportion of the terraces compared to when it attracted 10,000 spectators to a fixture and now the situation is compounded because they cannot even generate any additional revenues through the sales of refreshments and at the bars, since the landlords William Hill own these facilities. To compound this difficult situation, in the local area it's also "an unbelievably difficult job to bring in sponsorship", particularly when compared to local rivals Berwick[1] or tracks like visitors Somerset where "sponsorship levels are excellent". It is difficult to attract major financial support in Newcastle, which George notes, "is down to the place itself, as it's a major struggle to keep the sport going in the city, if your names not Newcastle United Football Club" where George himself, for his sins, is a season ticket holder! The speedway club attempt to compensate for this dearth of sponsors and interest by running lots of local promotions in an attempt to try to attract more people to visit the track with discounted tickets, school visits and, even that day, they'd been leafleting at an important motorcycle rally in Durham. These activities are not a magic solution, since the situation with school visits is extremely competitive and the speedway club finds itself disadvantaged in comparison to the school visits arranged by other local sports teams. The basketballers, for example, can easily put on a full display of their skills in a restricted space whereas the Diamonds can't even play their trump card – for understandable health, safety and noise reasons – because they daren't start up their demonstration bike at the school.

---

[1] though, in contrast to this opinion, parsimonious Berwick promoter Peter Waite claims it's impossible to attract high levels of sponsorship never mind to avoid running the Berwick club at anything other than a loss.

More resilient than downcast, George has high hopes for the next season when it's rumoured that speedway might restart at nearby Middlesbrough. This would provide a much-needed fillip to the interest of the fans as the club could, once again, race in local derby fixtures. It's an attraction and rivalry that doesn't exist with Berwick, presently the speedway club closest to them, which "technically isn't classed as a local derby". No matter whom the Diamonds are racing against, the "social element of the sport is fantastic" and George is fulsome in his praise of the "ability, skill and bravery of the riders". It's an admiration that's always there for George despite his caveat, gained through many years' work with riders in his official capacity as co-promoter, "even if you're dealing with them on a day-to-day basis". However, he does not doubt "their dedication", particularly as many of the riders are employed in full-time jobs away from their racing at the track. Throughout the country and particularly outside the Elite League, many riders are really only semi-professional participants in speedway, who all have to find the time and money to purchase and maintain their equipment. It's a lifestyle that contrasts markedly to those riders fortunate or skilled enough to ride full-time professionally and remains in sharp contrast to, and some wayward Newcastle players spring to my mind here, "other pampered sports stars". I'm grateful to George for his time, consideration and courtesy on another busy evening for him at Brough Park. I've just thanked him, when Somerset promoter Peter Toogood arrives in the office for a pre-meeting chat, but then apologises for his interruption, "oh, sorry, you're doing your thing, going down in history".

I leave the office and retreat briefly to the Somerset side of the pits where Jo Lawson, the Somerset co-promoter, chats with Sean Stoddart the 18-year-old Armadale rider, who clutches a Tesco's carrier bag. He's been drafted in for this fixture to help with the Somerset injury crisis that's already eliminated Chris Mills and Trevor Harding from reserve. Sean has been recommended as an exciting prospect to team manager Mick Bell by the referee who officiated at their Saturday night meeting at Berwick, when their ongoing injury jinx this time struck their replacement reserve Benji Compton. Sean is keen and hopes to impress as well as not succumb to the Somerset injury curse. He's very personable but dedicated to his long-term goal to try to "reach the top in speedway". Sean comes from Edinburgh, relishes the chance to ride for his local club at Armadale and is very definite that he's "always wanted to do this". He claims another stage in his long-term aim to pursue a successful career in the sport starts tonight, when he hopes to ride well and score points for Somerset in this Premier League meeting ("my ambition for tonight"). Sean has ridden for six years, although his advancement has been slightly hampered by the closure of Linlithgow after he had two seasons there, and the general "lack of tracks up north", though he practises wherever practicable and even goes for occasional spins on the beach at Portobello. He wouldn't have got to where he already is in speedway without "my dad and my mechanic", nonetheless, he remains a keen student of the sport and tries, wherever possible, to apply what he observes in the other riders around him in the pits and at meetings around the country. The riders that have most influenced him and fired his enthusiasm for the sport have been Hans Nielsen, Les Collins and, most recently, Rory Schlein. Just the experience to ride alongside Rory is education enough and, allied with Rory's real desire to educate and mentor Sean, it's all been really useful. "I think he's brilliant, a really nice guy and very helpful which says something about him, I think", declares Sean as he goes off to continue his education in the form of some last-minute instruction and individual advice from the experienced Somerset team manager, Mick Bell.

As a former rider, Mick knows the outlook and approach of riders, which helps him to motivate his own team as well as being able to pass on the many tricks and tactics of the trade. He appears a jovial presence in the pits and, when I pass a few minutes after he's offered some encouragement to Sean, he strolls round to speak to each Somerset rider in turn. His favourite initial question to them appears to be, "you been here before?"

The home grandstand and terraces begin to fill out nicely with quite a crowd of people, in eager anticipation of the fixture due to start in 45 minutes' time. There's also a gaggle of interested fans that crowd the white picket fence for a close look at the increased activity levels in the pits area. On the steps of the covered section of the terraces, in front of the steps that lead to the bar area, someone has hung a highly visible large Somerset flag. The marker pen text on the Rebels flag proclaims the undying allegiance of the flag's owners to the team and helpfully lists a few of the individuals who transported this flag to Newcastle. The Somerset fans have been on a road trip with the team and have suffered defeats at Edinburgh and Berwick, so far, but their enthusiasm remains undimmed. There are around 25 of them on the trip, who either stay on the caravan sites they booked in February or, if they're really lucky, at the same hotel that the team uses for the tour. Consequently there's great camaraderie among the contingent of riders, mechanics, co-promoters and fans as well as ample opportunity for them all to let their hair down together after the night's racing. Each night everyone has congregated in the pub by the Holiday Express in Berwick where the riders and some fans were billeted throughout the tour. In fact the Somerset riders, along with riders everywhere, are a sociable lot who are more than happy to spend some time to chat with their fans, even those riders who travel with their wives and children though these, perhaps, haven't had the same levels of resilience or availability when it comes to staying up to carouse the night away. The flag itself has travelled well and has held pride of place on the front of one of their caravans as they travel across the country. The sight of the flag has attracted considerable interest from other motorists on the road, who try to read it when it passes them ("it's getting the bus lots of looks"), and it has been a frequent talking point in the car parks and laybys that are an inevitable part of the numerous comfort breaks that long-distance journeys inevitably require. The flag continues to work its magic as it has now drawn my attention to the group of Rebels fans that loosely cluster around it.

There's quite a friendly, mixed group of people that includes 'Tim the Hat' – a large, very affable and knowledgeable man who wears the sort of magnificent hat that wouldn't look inappropriate on Screaming Lord Sutch. Away from the speedway he's a bookmaker and claims to be one of the (few) "honest ones", he's so sincere that you can't help but believe him. With him by the flag, rather territorially, are his friends from Taunton, notably 'Speedway Dave' – who jokes that he travels to "get away from the missus, but don't put that in or I'll be in trouble" – and the unmarried 'Johnny Sometimes' who, as the only member of the Caravan and Camping Club in the group, researched and booked the caravan sites in February when the 'Northern Tour' away fixtures were initially announced. The consensus is that they've "had a great time" and have only been too pleased to literally and metaphorically fly the flag for the club. They've had their photo taken in the pits with the riders (and the flag) "to show the boys we support them" and they hope this photograph will shortly appear in all its glory in a home match programme just to "show other people that there's fun to be had". Jo Lawson, the co-promoter, adds "we've had a good crowd with us on tour including a few Swindon ones, as they don't have a Northern Tour anymore". Despite the defeats, it's been an eventful and memorable trip with plenty of incidents and talking points to debate. The Edinburgh meeting featured ten fallers that included Paul Fry's spectacular doughnut fall in heat 7, executed with such aplomb that he still had the time to signal a congratulatory thumbs up to Ritchie Hawkins, who laid his bike down so promptly behind him. The young, rising Premier League potential star of the future Ritchie has one special fan on this trip, Margaret Hallett, who hails from near Andover but "always went to Swindon". She says simply, "Ritchie knows me as Supergran". She's absolutely besotted with him "he's my boy, my best friend" and has followed his career from the outset "since he was 15". He's patiently but skilfully worked his way up through the ranks after he started to ride competitively in the Conference League, so far with Mildenhall, Swindon, Berwick and now Somerset serves as the latest step on the route of his personal speedway apprenticeship.

The Somerset fans are a pleasantly mixed group of ages and gender which includes Di, who runs Magnus 'Zorro' Zetterstrom's Testimonial Stall and the 50/50 draw back at the track in Somerset, and Elaine who's been coming to speedway for 45 years. Di has really enjoyed the tour, "we've had a wonderful time and have laughed from the moment that we got in the car", plus there's been some enjoyable quality time spent with Zorro. He's "such a gentleman" although this is a view not held by the Berwick fans following "a coming together" with Tom P. Madsen last night. Everyone only has positive words about Zorro as a person, a rider and for what he's brought to the club this season. Di is positively evangelical on Zorro's behalf, since she views him as a "real team man" and, most significantly, as "one of speedway's nice guys". Events on track later in the evening would have most Newcastle fans question that analysis, but Di genuinely speaks as she finds based on considerable experience of the man on and off the track. 'Speedway Dave' interrupts loudly and mischievously to accuse Di of being overly obsessed with Zorro "every time he wins, you have an orgasm"; she smiles good-humouredly and replies with equanimity, " I'm just going to have to take him home with me". [2]

Di started going to speedway in 1960 when her "first boyfriend" was mechanic for Poole's captain Geoff Mudge. The relationship fizzled out but her love of the sport endures undimmed, which she puts rather elegantly, "the boyfriend lasted three months and the speedway 45 years so far". She has personally witnessed many changes to the sport she loves in the many intervening years from the heady time of her first love. The men in her own life may have come and gone, but the men racing on the track have been an abiding passion and always thrilling for Di. There have been considerable changes in the ranks of the riders and a huge shift in their approach and attitudes to the sport during this time. Contemporary speedway is "very much more professional"; the most notable change is that "gone are the days when they just threw their gear into the back of the truck and left it there until the next week". The riders themselves have always been good with the fans but, hand in hand with the decline in popularity of the sport, "you can now get closer to the riders than you could years ago". There's still a lack of "prima donnas" and, almost to a man throughout the sport, they're all great with the fans, "especially the Somerset riders". But amid all the praise, frivolity and bonhomie of the tour, it's also a trip heavily tinged with

<hr>

[2] I must stress that Di is not a Zorro groupie at all. In fact afterwards, Di is very keen that I clarify that she is "just someone to likes to get involved with speedway and help the riders by, for example, doing match reports for Zorro's website among many other things". I am very happy to make this clarification.

sadness – for Jo, Supergran and others – due to the premature death from cancer earlier in the week of Barbara, a dear speedway friend of the travelling Wiltshire contingent. The previous week at Somerset, Jo Lawson had spoken to me extremely glowingly about her friend and the sad news of her recent rapid decline in health. It was only a few days later that Barbara sadly passed away as a result of her illness, but only after a long and tenacious fight. The shock of her loss was still very raw to them all but it was clear that although she was gone from this earth, those who'd travelled away this weekend from Somerset on a tour of the northern speedway clubs did not forget her, let alone undervalue the good times they had enjoyed with her. They'd stood on the terraces with Barbara so often in the past; her absence in the future was going to be a continual reminder of her, just as it already was on this evening.

Since I'm at Brough Park to experience all things Newcastle Speedway, I soon leave the Somerset contingent to their own devices in order to sample the true flavour of the local fans that follow the Diamonds. I decide not to watch from behind glass in the tiered main grandstand and instead decide to view the meeting from near the back of the standing terraces surrounded by the many fans of the Diamonds.[3] The crowd around me features a general mix of ages with a noticeably high number of young women in addition to the usual preponderance of older males. I finally choose to stand by the steps that lead up to the bar, sandwiched between a middle-aged couple in front of me and another small group of 'typical' fans on the step behind me. There's the pensioner of the group, snappily dressed in a blue zip Regatta sweatshirt over his matching but unbuttoned collared shirt. Next to him is a tanned man

[3] At this point I must emphasise that Newcastle Speedway Club have always stood for something special in my view of the sport. Not only have I encountered George's mother Joan at away meetings in the past, most often at Reading, but also it was a fixture that featured Newcastle a few years ago at Workington that had the biggest impression on me. I particularly remember that day because there were a huge number of Workington fans as well as a large group of away supporters on the terraces. But, even more notably, there were a few fans of Newcastle Speedway Club who wore the usually hated red-and-white stripes of Sunderland Association Football Club and were able to mingle unselfconsciously among them without the inevitable rancour, bother or comment that this would usually attract. Though this might not be possible at home fixtures nor sensible to parade through the streets of Byker on the way to the meeting; it was, nonetheless, the ultimate counter example to the type of behaviour often experienced at football matches. It also exemplifies the fantastic behaviour and friendliness of which the sport of speedway is so justifiably proud. Large crowds of traditional (true) speedway fans exchange all the usual banter and criticism associated with passionate rivalry without the need to resort to violence or the need for police supervision, no matter how big the crowd or important the meeting. The sight of these Sunderland shirts was, for me, symbolic of the prevalence of this attitude in speedway and stood in sharp contrast to the narrow tribalism of contemporary football fanaticism which wouldn't tolerate this combustible combination of deeply held allegiances without the swift resort to violence.

who wears sunglasses throughout the meeting, despite a conspicuous lack of sunshine at the outset of the evening, which starts in some warmth under dull, overcast skies, and a smattering of darker rain clouds. Beside him is a blonde-haired young woman, dressed in pink sweatpants and Nike trainers, with a pink swoosh, offset by her NUFC replica shirt underneath her black sweatshirt and with an anorak tied around her waist. She's in her mid to late teens and I assume she is the daughter of the man in glasses and the granddaughter of the pensioner. Throughout the meeting they're all extremely vocal and keenly absorbed in the changing dynamics of each race, and their comments leave you in absolutely no doubt that they passionately want the Newcastle riders and team to prevail at all costs.

The Diamonds team has seen lots of recent changes in personnel. Following the acrimonious departure of Richard Juul from the side the week before, he's been replaced in the team not, as stated in the match programme, by Danish rider Henning Loof (who sounds like he's ready for use in a bathroom) but by Kristian Lund. His appointment captures the innate complexity of the rules and regulations that beset your average speedway team. It's a level of complexity that usually quickly defeats, forever, the attention span of even the most-determined novice spectator. In this case Kristian is a "Newcastle asset", which means that the Diamonds own his registration contract in the sport but, for the 2005 season, he'd already been loaned to Newport. The Wasps, according to the helpful explanation provided on the tannoy by announcer and co-promoter Barry Wallace, have kindly granted Newcastle permission to use their own rider as Juul's replacement for the rest of the season, since Newport no longer required Kristian's services. Even in a soothing Geordie accent, the minutiae of these rules remain shrouded in some confusion and mystery but this doesn't bother the young lady behind me. She enthusiastically screams her encouragement throughout each race to the home riders, but is particularly vocal with her shouts of "go on Kristian, go on, go on, Kristian". Her participation starts vociferously from heat 1 onwards. Not that you could miss Kristian when mounted on a speedway bike, as he appears a much 'bigger lad' than many others especially in comparison to the usual "70 to 80 kilos when wet" diminutive and jockeyesque stature of many speedway riders. I'm surprised he can't hear her shrieks of support, as she bounces from foot to foot, above the roar of the bikes and the muffling effect of his helmet. The pensioner with her adds his own repeated mantra of "get stuck into them, lad!" which he equally vehemently suggests albeit at a much lower decibel level.

Heat 2 witnesses the on-track re-appearance of former Diamond Rob Grant, who'd been loudly booed by the crowd on the introductory parade of the teams. He rides this race with his distinctive leg-trailing style that, though unusual, doesn't prevent him from remaining at the back of the race throughout this heat. In fact Rob, rather unfortunately but consistently, rides all three of his races badly trailed off at the rear. Heat 3 hears the announcer name-check the race sponsor (LH Pianotuning Ltd) with the touchingly old-fashioned observation that "if you need any tuning or repairs to your piano then the number is there to call". I'm sure that the general incidence of piano ownership has declined, in parallel with a similar deterioration of speedway attendances, since the height of its heyday and popularity in this country. Even if we assume there's still a burgeoning or latent demand for repairs, I'm not sure that the demographic of any speedway crowd would be your most obvious choice should you wish to target the remainder of the country's keen pianists. I admire the sponsor's optimism and continued support of their local speedway club though!

We often boast that speedway is a family sport and the group close by to me supports this claim with an accomplished display of coordinated family screams and shouts of "go on, go on" for Jamie Robertson in heat 5, perhaps they hope to watch a repeat of his wheelie celebration at the end of heat 4. The race line taken by Jamie Smith for second place, as they rush to the line from the final bend, provokes a hysterical reaction from Granddad who howls "you'll have him in the dog track you freaking dirty bastard". A few heats later one of the track staff also feels granddad's ire, who volunteers to freaking place a flag where the sun doesn't shine, for his tardy use of said flag when he eventually stopped heat 7. The level of anger the OAP possesses is almost palpable, unable to be held back from frequent eruptions start and is triggered by the most innocuous incidents. The start marshal is next to receive some harsh advice on his competence in heat 8, which sees the OAP freaking fulminate, once more, at Smith's lack of track etiquette when up against Robertson. "That's freaking twice Jamie boy" was the printable gist of his outburst. Just before the interval break, we're treated to Glenn Cunningham bravely pass Lubos Tomicek on an evening throughout which, as they say in match reports in the *Speedway Star*, 'passing was at a premium'.

Some of the small details I observe during the interval, I believe illustrate the essential charm of the sport. There's the young woman who is the Diamonds' team mascot and I spot her when she clacks down the stairs from the bar in her steel shoe and red kevlars while she eats her interval portion of chips with gusto. We're informed by Barry, the Geordie announcer, that Roy Clarke, mechanic for the Diamonds' heat leader James Grieves, has a spare place in his van for Thursday night's trip to Sheffield, leaving from Palmerston, should anyone wish to make themselves known to him at the pits gate to make arrangements during the interval. Barry even has the time to wonder aloud whether Andrew Dalby, the Sunderland AFC season-ticket holding centre-green announcer, will have the time during his busy interval schedule to snatch a well-earned interval cuppa? We then learn from Andy that, while he mostly tries to live life on the edge, he "can't stand coffee flavour and has only had two cups of tea in 16 years!"

Immediately after the interval, the meeting quickly moves onto a more controversial plane with the events of the very next heat. Even before it has started, granddad vociferously advises Grievesy with some slightly obtuse and unorthodox tactics – "go on Jimmy put him on the freaking green grass!" – to deal with the threat posed by Zorro in this race. The whole thing kicks off and anger levels rise exponentially when Zorro, who trails in this race by some distance in second place behind Christian Henry, appears to decide to deliberately knock him off with a charge on a straight line that takes him directly underneath him on bends 3 and 4 of lap 3. In my view, it's a manoeuvre that was never likely to result in anything other than its actual outcome, which is that Henry and his machine smash dramatically and painfully into the wire safety fence. James Grieves skilfully lays down his bike to avoid the fallen riders ahead of him before he immediately jumps to his feet and, in the heat of the moment demonstrates the skill that once made him a boxer, when he punches Zorro in the face a few times through the narrow gap provided for this very purpose at the front of his helmet. The track staff just about manage to hold the riders back from further violent confrontation, with Zorro particularly keen to break free of his handlers to effect some swift retribution on the always-up-for-it Grieves, while the medical staff crowd round the stricken Henry. The partisan crowd of locals have gone ballistic while granddad, rightly for once, fulminates to all and sundry around him as he repeatedly shrieks, "he had freaking ne' chance of getting past him there". Grieves ostentatiously apologises to Zorro with a proffered handshake as they depart via the centre green on the long trudge back to the pits from the bend on the far end of the stadium. Henry still lies prostrate on the track as the medical staff and ambulance crowd round him in attendance. His injuries could have been much more serious than they were, nonetheless, it's still an incident that ends his season for 2005 there and then. The crowd hasn't had this formally confirmed at the time, but it's a reasonable assumption given the severity with which he hit the fence, which is a particularly galling outcome when his recent improved form on the track is considered. Subsequently we learn that the injuries Christian sustains from the crash result in a huge gash on his thigh, right through to the bone, which is then initially stitched together albeit with the strong possibility of future skin grafts if it fails to properly heal.

The SCB referee, Workington-based Stuart Wilson, summons the riders, Grieves and Zetterstrom – and the team managers, English and Bell – to the changing rooms for an impromptu emergency discussion. The crowd has massed by the pits fence where they bay for retribution and, to be polite, are calling provocatively to everyone involved with the Somerset team. The atmosphere has taken on a nasty, violent edge – restricted to verbal threats but that I sense would quickly translate to physical action, if further 'provoked' – while the pits wall provides a welcome barrier for the Somerset riders still stuck in the pits. Peter Toogood forlornly stands alone. He looks completely downcast and nonplussed. It's a tricky situation for him, politically and presentationally, since he's both the co-promoter of the Somerset team as well as being Chairman of the BSPA, speedway's governing body. He resolves the dilemma of his position through a sustained campaign of total inaction and remains apparently completely detached on the periphery of the incident and its aftermath throughout the rest of the evening. It's as though he's not there or just an accidental bystander in a bad dream. We're all interrupted by the announcer who ecstatically proclaims that Christian is "back on his feet and able to walk past the ambulance" apparently intent to walk back to the pits unaided before, after a few tentative steps, commonsense prevails and he's helped into the ambulance. The crowd by the pits fence continue to bate the Somerset riders and go deliriously potty with extended jeers, when Zorro emerges, or more accurately, storms from the changing rooms to animatedly speak with Peter Toogood in a flurry of ferocious waves and assorted other arm gestures. No further details have been confirmed about the referee's decision on this incident, other than his initial award of the race to Henry and Zorro's subsequent exclusion, to loud cheers, for "foul riding" although the fact that Zorro angrily starts to pack his equipment away seems to speak for itself. The announcer Barry tries to restore calm and counsels the still wild home crowd with a peculiar choice of advice, "a message to Newcastle fans: don't take it out on the Somerset fans as, whatever you thought you saw on the track, wasn't them and isn't the sort of behaviour we want at a speedway meeting". Soon after we learn, to a roar of approval from the Diamonds fans, that there has been a "rare referee's decision to exclude him [Zorro] from the rest of the meeting". [4]

[4] a few days later I'm told anecdotally that Stuart Wilson, the referee in question, had previously witnessed, in his capacity as a spectator, Zorro's involvement in a similar incident when Zorro "accidentally speared" a rival rider, after he inadvertently crossed the grass of the bend. The decision of the referee that day, unlike at Newcastle, was to put all four riders back in for the re-run of the race. The subsequent print and Internet furore that surrounded this episode in Newcastle was exacerbated by a debate as to whether referees should punish apparent unfair or rough riders and their riding with fines and exclusions or ignore these incidents as just part and parcel of a dangerous sport. It is a debate that will continue. Though, equally, I imagine that now the metaphorical dam has been breached, that we will see more SCB referees take strong, decisive action in the future.

I leave the still angry crowd by the pits fence to rejoin the group of Somerset fans who stand on the grandstand terraces to establish their impressions on this train of events. When I arrive Tim the Hat, the most visible fan in their group, informs me that he was disturbed to be approached immediately after the incident, by an extremely angry man in a black-and-white cap (whom he points out to me staring back at us from about 10 yards away and I'm relieved to notice isn't the perpetually angry pensioner I stood with) who threatened him with violent retribution. Tim rather plaintively asks if I "saw the abuse we were getting?" or was close enough by to have possibly heard the threat of "I'm going to shank you afterwards" from the brute in the cap. The threat of violence, compounded by the broad Geordie accent of the very intimidating man as well as anxiety over the specific intention behind the forceful use of the word "shank", is an extremely worrying development for the group of Somerset fans, who huddle still closer together as a group. Tim assumed these comments specifically referred to a definite intention to threaten his person afterwards, though whether the man was to punch or stab him no one could accurately predict but, nonetheless, everyone had a reasonably good idea that a post-meeting cuddle hadn't been proposed.

Rather than pour oil on already troubled waters, Tim sensibly sought out Barry the announcer to inform him of what had been said, if not so far transpired. Barry, with commendable alacrity, promptly tried to calm things and assuage the heightened tension of the situation among some members of the home crowd, when he broadcast an appeal for general tolerance ("the Somerset fans aren't responsible for what goes on out on the track and shouldn't be held responsible by anyone"). Di, the big Zorro fan, is outraged by the decision of the referee about this "racing incident" and indignantly says, "I've never heard of that before, I don't understand that – we should withdraw". Di's considered opinion of the event we'd all witnessed was very definite, "Magnus would never take a fellow rider out on purpose, he's not that kind of rider, riders have to take split-second decisions and he took the wrong one". Beside her, Margaret is more philosophical, "well it gives us something to talk about going home" but, then, she can comfortably say that since it's an incident that doesn't involve her beloved Ritchie. Speedway Dave believes that the ref is a confirmed practising onanist and another Somerset fan says "we all have a word for him". While co-promoter Jo looks to the practical implications of events and feels that this rare decision has "taken away the chance of a bonus point". The remainder of the Somerset fans in this small group also appear to be nonplussed by this surprise turn of events. Despite a couple of centuries' speedway attendance between them, no one can recall any other rider ever being thrown out of meeting in modern times for such an incident, especially for an occurrence that isn't exactly uncommon within the sport. The jungle drums continue to still beat strongly and the collective memory has been consulted, which is illustrated when a text message to Elaine arrives from the former Rebels' team manager Ray Dickson. He now organises the juniors in the second halves at Somerset and, Elaine reports the gist of his text message, namely that as an "ex-Monarchs' supporter" he's "never seen (sic) such a thing since Charlie Monk and Doug Templeton were thrown out at Edinburgh in the 1960s".

By the nominated race of heat 15, a 5–1 would give Newcastle the opportunity to win by 24 points and thereby force a run-off for the bonus point. Josef 'Pepe' Franc falls on bend 1, apparently without help, but the referee calls all four riders back, due to his view that it was an unsatisfactory start. It's noticeable throughout the meeting that while Franc's name is spelt in a way that would lead you to think that you should pronounce it like the coin, his surname is actually pronounced like the country at Brough Park and, subsequently it transpires, in Josef's home country of the Czech Republic. Whatever the pronunciation it makes no difference because 'Pepe' storms to an easy victory in the re-run of heat 15, followed home in second place by his team-mate James Grieves. On his subsequent victory celebration lap, Franc delightedly stops in front of the home grandstand and takes a theatrical bow. Almost simultaneously, the third-placed Somerset rider Paul Fry reacts dramatically to physically attack James Grieves just at the moment when he arrives at the pits gate after his celebration lap. The crowd storms en masse over towards the pits area for a better view of this altercation and in the ensuing confusion it's difficult to see or establish what exactly is happening. Although it's clear that there's an almighty rumpus and that the barney mostly involves Fry and Grieves who ferociously attack each other with considerable gusto. When the dust of another fight finally settles, Grieves returns to his section of the pits to receive, what is effectively a victor's welcome from the nearby, baying Newcastle fans. Despite his diminutive stature, Grieves (who used to train to improve his upper body strength with kick boxing) strides with bantam-like confidence around the pits area, even though he has a remarkably prominent lump on his forehead – reputedly sustained as a result of a kick in the head from Paul Fry's mechanic. Which, if this was achieved while he was still astride his bike, signals a possible impressive alternative career in ballet should a ban from mechanic's duties result from these (alleged) actions.

Whatever has prompted these scenes – rumoured to be Paul Fry mistaking Grieves's "innocent celebratory hand gestures" as a deliberate and provocative form of personal insult – it's obvious that tensions continue to run extremely high on both sides of the pits. A Newcastle fan close by suggests that the only sensible option is to "give 'em boxing gloves and let them settle it on the centre green" Diamonds co-promoter George English sensibly swiftly steps in to admonish Grieves and to stop him from playing up to the assembled crowd at the pits fence perimeter; while his mother, Joan, restores a good degree of order with her loud instructions to the many trespassers to relocate themselves with considerable speed or risk injury and expulsion. Although she is small and much older than everyone who surrounds her, Joan quickly restores a semblance of order and control with her powerful presence and voice. The referee Stuart Wilson again returns to the pits area for another long discussion with Mick Bell, this time in full view of the crowd rather than hidden away in the intimate privacy of the dressing rooms.

While tensions still run high on both sides, there's still the final drama of the run-off for the bonus point to unfold between the riders nominated by the rival team managers. In this instance, we are to see a match race between Josef 'Pepe' Franc and Ritchie Hawkins. The tension is all too much for Supergran who tosses her programme board to the floor and shoots off saying, "I just can't watch it, I just can't watch it". Tim the Hat is the voice of understanding and compassion, when he sweetly says to her in a calm voice, "come on Nana, come on Nana". We gather that Supergran is anxious that if Ritchie were to win the run-off, she's anxious that this might spark further aggravation in the pits and on the terraces.

The selection of Pepe is not a surprise choice, since he has remained completely unbeaten by a visiting rider all night. Before this decisive race can even start, the Newcastle start marshal decides to indulge himself in some apparent last-minute gamesmanship, when he unnecessarily harasses Hawkins at the tapes about the inaccuracy of his starting position on the recently repainted white lines of the start grid. Again George English intervenes, in his role as co-promoter, mediator and true sportsman, when he runs over to overrule these petty concerns, and thereby enables the race to start and Pepe to zoom away confidently to win in untroubled style. Just as the race finishes, the Newcastle riders run on the track in celebration to give Pepe the bumps for his performance and also an early, very unexpected bath, to judge from his reaction, when they duck him in the handily adjacent centre-green pond. Announcer Barry, for once without the hyperbole that naturally afflicts the species, intones his closing summary of events, "an extraordinary last hour or so at Brough Park for one of the most eventful meetings I've ever seen at a speedway track!" before he finishes with considerable understatement, "so, in the light of circumstances, there won't be a victory parade". Supergran has finally returned to the Somerset group, while they pack away their flag, flaks and sandwich boxes in preparation to leave the stadium, with tears in her eyes from the emotion and upset of it all which, culminated for her, in the drama of Ritchie's run-off race. She's in determined and ebullient mood about his career prospects though, despite the set back of the last race, "I've seen him get a maximum in the Conference League, I've seen him get a maximum in the Premier League and I'll be on my Zimmer frame when I see him get a maximum in the Elite League!"

The home crowd cheerfully swarms to the bar, continues to mill and mass round the pits area or streams out of the stadium. I catch a preoccupied but satisfied George English for his immediate thoughts a few minutes later. "All I will say is that personally I thought Zetterstrom totally deserved to be thrown out. However, I want a definitive list of fines from the referee before I comment further, as fines were being dished out all around earlier". In front of the grandstand I chat to Paul and Karen Brown from Northumberland who are one of many groups who hang around and talk about events animatedly, in their case with their children. They've "never seen anything like it before" but don't really wish to be drawn on any specific comments, though there's absolutely no doubt that they hold Zorro to blame for the fights that marred the meeting (even though he'd left in his van before the second contretemps). They watch all the speedway that they can as family, on TV, at Brough Park or at the British Grand Prix in Cardiff. Their daughter Lauren, and her friend Bethan, are both professed James Grieves fans and appear quite shocked by events that involved their hero. The unusual events of the evening haven't in any way deterred her brother Sean, who "likes everything" about the sport, from the desire to fulfil his ambition to "become a speedway rider". His dad prefers to sound a note of caution and concentrate on matters that specifically impact the current form of the Diamonds, since he believes that "George needs to think long and hard" about rider selection, particularly since "he's dropped a few clangers recently". Paul hopes that the poor crowds might pick up in the future, especially if there was a more attractive team to watch race at Brough Park. He welcomes the increased TV coverage on Sky Sports, but it doesn't, to his mind, change the fundamental fact that, "it's never been a big sport, it's always been a poor man's sport". His wife Karen nods her approval throughout as she listens to her husband, though she personally loves the atmosphere and the thrills of speedway. As they leave the stadium, Paul declares, "if I won the lottery I'd take over Newcastle!"

I wander back off through the deserted stadium and join the many fans already in the glass-fronted grandstand bar, who animatedly relive the evening's events in blow-by-blow fashion over a pint. I wave to George and notice that the referee, Stuart Wilson, sits completely isolated and alone in another deserted part of the stand, while he painstakingly completes his official report for the SCB on the night's tumultuous events. Given all that we witnessed, you just know that he's going to struggle to describe all the incidents and list all the fines never mind finish the remainder of the paperwork quickly!

Just after 9 p.m., I trundle off into the dusk of the evening that envelopes the Byker estate, with the sky decorated with wisps of glowing red clouds, many hours after the start of a memorable meeting that will be talked about for years afterwards, particularly when it becomes ever more dramatic in the recollection. A short distance away at Byker Metro Station, unusually to my mind, there are two police squad cars with flashing emergency lights parked directly outside on the entrance concourse. I worry that there has been some kind of emergency or terrorist incident. But, instead, more mundanely discover that the vestibule of the station is guarded by three policemen, well, one of them was actually a policewoman, each of them dramatically armed with a sub-machine gun (!) and spread out across this part of the completely silent and deserted station. I'm concerned enough to ask, "Is there something wrong, officer?" "No, it's just a bit of high visibility policing to reassure the public." I'm not convinced because just the mere sight of these impressive guns makes me nervous. To disguise my anxiety, I inform them that we could have done with their armed presence at the speedway fixture at Brough Park tonight. The tallest policeman replies, without discernable irony, "I thought they always knocked seven bells out of each other on the track and then had a punch up after!" before he adds, " Are you saying it's not like that every week at the speedway?" Just for tonight, I can't possibly disagree with him.

14th August 2005 Newcastle v Somerset (Premier League) 60–36

Chapter Four – Plymouth

Apart from the fewer vans parked up inside the stadium already, when I arrive back at the St Boniface Arena riders entrance gate there's a ground-hog day déjà vu all over again type feel. That said, the dress code is definitely much smarter. Mike Bowden's daughter Ruth looks ready for a smart upscale dinner party while her father eschews his casual clothes in favour of a more dashing dark jacket with prominent BSPA badge set off by a collared shirt and tie. Away from her speedway race-night duties, Ruth works in Social Services contracting. She's well used to negotiation, people management and a demanding work environment that requires working to tight deadlines. She handles the arriving riders, mechanics and officials with friendly but firm diplomacy. Her father is never too busy to pop back to check what happens and isn't reluctant to offer advice, "He's like Blakey – you gotta know how to handle him!" Ruth is an articulate conversationalist and takes a refreshingly matter-of-fact view of life, "We only know a fraction of what goes on. We kid ourselves about our place in the universe. We need seven hours sleep a night and should drink two litres of water a day but, beyond that, we're all mammals really!" Ruth knows her way round motorbikes but resists the inclination to parade her knowledge or to get caught up in the tittle-tattle or gossipy backbiting that's sometimes the lingua franca of the riders' van car park prior to (and after) a meeting. "I don't care what the speedway riders earn or don't earn. If it's £8 or £800, its their decision what they risk for that! They're doing a job where they could end up in a wheelchair for whatever they're paid! I wouldn't do it!" Ruth's sister Angela interjects, "She used to mechanic for Mike from the age of seven." Ruth makes light of her extensive experience, "I used to do everything for him." Angela adds, "She don't watch anymore, like me. Dad used to take us everywhere."

Though most riders are already here, a stream of vehicles draw up to the entrance gate. Man of many hats but questionable ability, Weymouth chairman, promoter and team manager, Phil Bartlett arrives in a sleek American styled black large-sized people carrier notable for its alloy wheels and personalised number plate. Effectively, it's the after version of a white van after an appearance on *Pimp My Ride*. Roomy enough for many large sized passengers, tonight Mr Bartlett arrives with Weymouth's presenter and webmaster Tim Helm and charming ex-Wimbledon but latter-day Wildcats speedway fan Allen Boon, Snr. (but, sadly, without Phil's glamorous logo-loving partner and Wildcats Ace commercial head honcho, Samantha Knight). Allen is 73 next week but remains, even after many decades watching speedway, as engaged and enthusiastic about the sport as ever. "We had brilliant racing last night at Weymouth. Some races you could have thrown a blanket over all four riders! Adam McKinna fell off – bits flying off his bike and that – and got straight up. Whereas Dan Halsey fell off and he was on the track for 20 minutes and got carried off to hospital! It all depends on how you fall, doesn't it?"

My book display table is in a similar place as earlier for the GB Under-15 Championships. It's strategically located a short distance away from the entrance turnstiles and programme stall en route towards the toilet block, pits area, trackshop and, of course, the track. Vendor Noah is on the table adjacent to my left – selling *Speedway Stars* and *Speedway Star* calendars – while to his left DVD man David Hawking sets out his DVD stall prior to going off to film the meeting. Noah initially sells a few *Speedway Stars* from the bundle he has in front of him until Mike Bowden comes over to exchange a few harsh words (that I don't properly catch because I'm chatting) and remove the unsold remainder of the bundle from him. When I ask Noah why Mike's so narked, he explains gnomically, "He's not happy cos I took a couple of these off." Noah flourishes date coded barcodes torn from the front of the *Speedway*

Star's he sold. Noah shrugs off this angry exchange to continue to meet and greet pretty well every passer by, irrespective of whether or not he tries to sell them a copy of the *Speedway Star* 2011 calendar.

With his hair gelled into his distinctive ginger bed-head style, trademark sunglasses and an untucked white collared shirt (without tie) that would make him feel cold later if he were less hard, Phil Bartlett wanders from the vicinity of his expensively sleek parked vehicle with some pre-meeting fried food bought from one of the St Boniface Arena refreshment stalls (that earlier some Plymouth fans advised me against). Noah calls out cheerily, "You're going to win tonight, Phil!" Phil doesn't seem keen to stop by for a chat but does call back, "I dunno, we'll see!" While Phil strides purposefully off to the pits with a confidence that belies his lack of tactical speedway team management acumen, Noah remains sure that the Wildcats will put up a good performance. "They've got a good side with McKinna and Cockle! What do you think of René Bach then? I think it'll be a Newcastle versus Edinburgh final. It should be really exciting! Newcastle have Dakota North, Mark Lemon and Kenni Larsen too. Edinburgh have Ryan Fisher and he's awesome!" Judged by the way that the Plymouth Devils were late to embrace the worldwide web and, until they got their latest website, were then reluctant to update it – you could be forgiven for thinking that Internet usage wasn't a big priority for those affiliated with the club or its officials. Definitely bucking the trend within the older generation speedway community, Noah is from a younger different digital generation, so embraces its search and social networking possibilities enthusiastically. So much so that Noah prefers to comment widely online rather than restrict his opinions on all things speedway solely to his Facebook account. Apropos of nothing Noah tells me, "I've put on my Facebook page that I hope Matt Bates breaks his leg." Given that Matt rides at No. 3 for the Devils, my assumption is that Noah must have some sort of theatrical background, "What to wish him good luck like they do before plays?" In fact, Noah has no theatrical intention, "What's that?"

My explanation of theatrical superstition is cut short by ex-Exeter Falcons promoter, David Short who is here tonight having recently rediscovered his love of speedway. "I did some team management here and some other things but, not being involved, I drifted away but I've come back now! I go to Plymouth and Somerset. People are upset, like I am, about Exeter speedway but they don't believe me when I say Colin [Hill] didn't leave enough to reintroduce the sport! Nor are they happy when I blame English Nature!" No trip to Plymouth speedway would be complete for me without a chat to Paul 'Grizzly' Adams. However, tonight it's going to have to be since he's not here. Luckily, I'm able to catch up with his sister Julie Rickard and her daughter Laura. They're both fanatical Devils fans though Laura's speedway attendance has to fit round the demands of her Egyptology and Ancient History degree at the University of Swansea. Nonetheless, she still packs in a lot of speedway over the summer, despite the intrusion of a successful re-sit. She enjoys university life but prefers the convenience and predictability of living on campus in Halls of Residence, ("I've moved from room number 13, to 15, to 5 and now I've moved to number 23"). Contrary to press reports and the attendance figures released by the organisers, Laura believes that the attendance at the Cardiff Speedway Grand Prix declined in 2010. "I thought the crowd was less this year – there were definitely no Poles! The racing was really good though!"

Though the result of tonight's meeting will make no real difference to the overall standing of either side in the final National Trophy table, the bragging rights any local derby between these two teams bestows ensures there's a buzz about the place. With racing not too far off, quite a queue of fans still have yet to come through the turnstiles. Once inside, some fans linger to consider whether to buy a book, calendar, or DVD but, mostly, they trundle off to their favourite spot within the stadium grounds. To the right of my table the back doors of Seemond Stephens's van remain open. Sat on its sill are a gentleman and Seemond Stephens's mum. She tightly holds the leads of two small dogs dressed in smart bright coats with Asian style patterns. It's news to Seemond's mum that her son is now Plymouth's all-time top points scorer. When I mention this fact to Laura Rickard, she already knows but can, with absolutely no hesitation, recite Pete Lansdale's vital statistics.

The calm of this pleasant September evening suddenly ends in a commotion at the table next to me after a man in a baseball cap worn the wrong way round draws attention when he raises his voice with Noah. The gentleman is clearly angry and their age, size, height and weight difference is instantly noticeable. With his back to me, the man holds his face a fraction of an inch from Noah's in the manner of prize boxers at a press launch. Some further passionate but indistinct discussions ensue where both parties give a full and frank exchange of opinion. People watch but don't intervene. Instead, like myself, they just stand and gawp – whether they're at the programme stall, stood close by, queuing to get in, sat on the back of their van, run over from other parts of the St Boniface Arena or are in the substantial sized gaggle of fans stood on the mound that, when they face in the other direction, overlooks bends one and two. Discussions soon predictably escalate into muted (unreciprocal) violence the onlookers anticipate. The gentleman knocks Noah dramatically to the ground with a blow to the face. Unprepared to concede whatever points they discuss, Noah gets up, stares wilfully at his attacker only to then be knocked to the floor again with a loud slap. Though Noah's quick up onto his feet – to stand stock still in true Audley Harrison fashion – almost as rapidly, he's again knocked to the floor by the force of the next blow. Noah looks shaken (with a red cut-cum-weal on his cheek from the blows) but insolent while the gentleman remains extremely angry. Keen to continue this confrontation, despite the studious lack of resistance from Noah, the gentleman is suddenly held back by a chap in a fluorescent sleeveless jacket and a traditionally worn Devils cap. Close by, a visibly angry Gary Spiller is also held back while, in almost cartoon caricature fashion, he smoulders like a tractor tyre on a farm bonfire. Gary doesn't advance any further towards Noah's table of calendars but expresses his extreme rage via wildly flung arm movements.

The reaction of the majority of people is just to stand and watch the drama unfold but, almost as soon as the man in the fluorescent jacket calls a halt to this sudden mismatched bout of animus, urgent conversations all around break the silence. Probably dazed, Noah runs off in the direction of the programme booth to find his mum, Alison. Strangely, all of a sudden, everyone's got an opinion as well as expertise and insight. Unconfirmed reports indicate that Noah is a zealous online communicator, albeit not with a volume that would put him in Derek Barclay's league. Noah's allegedly posted various messages about Matt Bates, Mark Simmonds (and close relations) as well as supposedly impersonating Gary Spiller on the speedway update site in a manner calculated to draw negative attention. Given I only look at the results on the updates (rather than bathe in the perspicacity of the posts) and don't belong to Facebook, I'm unaware of anyone's postings, let alone those made by or allegedly attributed to Noah.

Clearly Noah's social networking activities prompt great ire in some quarters. Alison and her sister Ruth initially try to resolve the situation by enlisting the help of their father Mike Bowden to resolve Ken Bates's confrontation with Noah. However, with no joy from that quarter, they report this confrontation to the police who are now said to be on their way to the stadium. Without the context of Noah's alleged online activities, contrary to detective dramas on the telly, all anyone can reasonably report is the events they saw (if they did see them or chose to say they saw them). The reportable event effectively started when both parties locked their heads close together by the display table of *Speedway Star* calendars. My own impression is that Noah offered no physical resistance, let alone threw a punch. In high dudgeon, Ruth appears by my table to ask rhetorically, "What sort of man hits a 17-year old? What sort of sport condones this sort of thing? My dad don't want to know! Gary Spiller's in the pits getting statements saying Noah threw the first punch!" Ruth turns to Seemond Stephens's mum who's still sat in the doorway of her son's van, "So you just sat there and watched a 17-year old get hit?" She replies, "I was looking after my dogs! I'm a 65-year old woman. What was I supposed to do?" The arrival of a police car and police van prompts Ruth to leave us. "What does she think I should do? He was lucky it was only three."

Rather than the aggressive style of policing style often seen on television shows like *Starsky & Hutch* or *The Sweeney*, the Devon

Constabulary appear to operate in the modern low-key friendly manner, possibly in order to diffuse any lingering tension but also to maximise the information they gather. They arrive comparatively mob-handed in a police car and a police van – possibly under the mistaken impression that there could be a need to take quite a few people down the station to help them with their enquiries. Ruth pops over to state rhetorically, "Noah said that you saw what happened – you will be making a statement! Won't you?" A policeman and a blonde-haired policewoman soon arrive at my book display table to take down my basic particulars. They emphasise that they intend to continue to question all and sundry in order to establish/investigate exactly what just happened between the two protagonists inside the stadium. They promise to return in 15 minutes to take a statement. Moments after they leave in the direction of the pits, Graham Reeve passes walking quickly in the opposite direction en route for the car park. I call out to Graham for advice. "Like I've already told the police, I'm just a speedway fan close to the fracas. I'd prefer that any dispute could be amicably resolved without violence and or the involvement of the police." Many other potential witnesses quickly melt into the anonymity of the crowd. Given the proximity of my table to Noah's stall, it's impossible to deny the claims of others that I was a well-placed witness to this incident. Graham's definite that the rule of law should be upheld, although he's not personally going to stay around to uphold it! "Say what you saw! Call me next week and I'll fill you in on what's really happening!"

Rob Peasley pops to my table enervated by the incident, "The police will definitely be wanting to take your statement!" Fifteen minutes later instead of the return of the two officers, PC Harrip (Badge No. 6923) arrives to take my statement. Prior to doing so I inform him that I'd prefer not to make a statement and request his advice on what detail to include in the light of rumours that others intend to make statements that directly contradict my account. Rather than answer my questions, PC Harrip points to a small object on the breast of his jacket and says, "Just to let you know that everything you're saying has been filmed and recorded."

[Jeff] "Shouldn't you have told me that before we started?"

[PC Harrip] "I'm telling you now!"

PC Harrip effects surprise that I could believe that he had a legal obligation to inform me that he would film and record my conversation prior to doing so. Clearly I'm no expert on the law but it seems highly likely that prior permission should be sought and warning given. While, I fully understand that the recording evidence allows the police force to corroborate statements taken from witnesses in the likelihood of later dispute, this 'accidental' use of his equipment illustrates why some people don't automatically trust the integrity of the police. Contrary to my expectations and unlike television drama, PC Harrip laboriously writes out my comments longhand. Luckily for him, albeit in rapidly fading light, he has my book display table to rest on. Behind us the speedway meeting gets underway. Though I can hear the roar of the bikes, to all intents and purposes it might as well take place on the moon for all the attention I give it. Hardly satisfactory after a long trip here from Brighton. The meeting is a stop-start affair with a substantial delay for a crash in heat 2. PC Harrip's future career as a dictation secretary might be hampered by both his lack of shorthand and his laborious handwriting. Inevitably, if regularly taking statements, an element of précis is involved. It's also a given that PC Harrip's familiarity with the language used and/or required by the courts dictates that he uses slightly stilted much more formal phrases than those of everyday conversation. Nonetheless, it's still a surprise that his word choice is a greater factor in 'my statement' – of events that I rather than he witnessed – than I'd expect. With hindsight and in the cold light of day, it's very easy for people to ignore the explicit and implicit pressure of this slightly fraught situation and say, 'well, don't sign it'.

PC Harrip sets to his task in dedicated fashion. He tends towards the noncommittal and aloof rather than the friendly. Probably an understandable reaction to a routine task in darkening unfamiliar surroundings. Either way, there's limited small talk except for his observation, "You're an Aries!" Fading light isn't the only extraneous element to impinge on PC Harrip's intense concentration as he writes out the statement since we're continually interrupted by other people keen to put over their tuppence worth (but not make a statement). While they can't influence this statement, they're certainly keen to provide additional context. Noah's mum Angela is one of the first to approach us and she tells PC Harrip, "He deserves locking up!" PC Harrip is polite but firm, "Could you go away – I'm trying to take a statement here!" Shortly afterwards Angela's wish to a certain extent comes true when police officers escort Ken Bates out of the stadium by police officers.[1] It's not long before another man comes up to tell PC Harrip, "He wanted hitting a long time ago." With a vague hint of exasperation, PC Harrip politely but firmly says, "Please go away!" Yet another man comes up to offer PC Harrip the use of his torch. "Nah, it's okay, thank you." Like everyone else who interrupts, this man also has a strong opinion, "He's had it coming for some time and totally deserved it." PC Harrip remains polite ("Thank you") but continues to write.

Keen to record my statement in the language of the court, PC Harrip insists on calling the incident "an assault" whereas I'm keen to stress that I identify it as "a fracas". We take a considerable time over the statement and, while I can hear the meeting continue, frustratingly I can't watch it. In fact, by this time we can't see much at all until a second policeman comes along to shine a torch on the many pages of the statement. Again, I stress that I don't want to escalate or even intervene in the situation. After the statement is read back, slightly amended and signed, PC Harrip gives me an information leaflet produced for the Criminal Justice System entitled "You've reported a crime ... so what happens next?" What happens next is I'm told I'll almost certainly hear nothing about this ever again. What then happens next is that the police leave the stadium to go and sit in their car outside for quite some time (to discuss matters unknown).

Spat out after my involuntary but tangential brief encounter with the early stage workings of the judicial system, in darkness I pack up my

[1] Ex-Weymouth photographer and press officer Julie Martin rings me the next day with news on this arrest. "All charges were dropped – it was self-defence! Adam has some serious problems!"

table and books. By the time, I wander up onto the banked area that overlooks the first bend, unfortunately (for me) heat 8 is already over in this Plymouth versus Weymouth National Trophy meeting. Against all predictions, Weymouth flew into an early 10-2 lead but, according to most accounts, Phil Bartlett's tactical and strategic ineptitude marshalling the rider resources available to him effectively ruins any chance of a Wildcats victory. Rather than linger on the cool terraces, I make my way to the pits in order to (hopefully) chat to promoter Mike Bowden about the events of the evening. Sadly he's nowhere to be seen so I ask a morose-looking man with the words "Machine Examiner" written on his shirt, "How come the pits seems so deserted?"

[Man] "Everyone is pissed off in the pits. Well 95%! It's shit!

[Jeff] "Where is Mike?"

[Man] "On the centre green."

[Jeff] "Where is Gary Spiller then?"

[Man] "On the centre green."

[Jeff] "Everyone's on the centre green?"

[Man] "Some wish they weren't here at all!"

Standing on the centre green at the farthest point away from the pits area in the vicinity of the third bend, possibly isn't the ideal location from which to manage and or motive the Plymouth Devils riders. However, it is a tricky spot for curious policemen to reach easily. Moments later as I stomp away from the stadium Graham Hambly issues an appeal over the

---

² On the British Speedway Forum, Rob Peasley notes, "It was only just completed in time before the 9.30 p.m. curfew, after a number of reruns in the opening races, with Ben Reade getting well and truly entangled in the safety fence after picking up drive in heat 2 and ending up with a foot injury. Weymouth looked hot favourites to win early on taking a 10-2 lead but with Simmonds and Stephens both unbeaten, Plymouth had the match won with a heat to spare and could afford to keep their maximum men out of the final heat in which the Wildcats took a consolation 5-1. Some weird team management from Weymouth with trump card Gary Cottham, given reserve rides in all the wrong places; some good action with Nicki Glanz, Jamie Pickard (who's improved no end since I last saw him) and Tom Brown, all producing some good passes. The Plymouth track has improved a lot since my last visit in 2007." In his report for the *Speedway Star*, Graham Hambly comments, "Plymouth recovered well from a disastrous start". In the same issue, promoter Mike Bowden offers some praise. "The referee and officials did well to see that the remaining 12 races were completed in an hour [after Ben Reade's crash caused extensive damage to the safety fence]. It was a good win for us despite being down to a six-man team and proved to be a very entertaining and exciting meeting."

stadium loudspeaker, "Would Gary Spiller please come to the pits as soon as possible?" Without being on hand to witness it, it's impossible to know whether Gary's return is a request from his riders, officials or the police. If there's any lesson to learn from tonight then it's always best to bring a jumper if you expect it to be cool later. It's also a good idea not to comment on situations you don't witness or hear and, even if you do, it's not always easy to exactly recall these for a written statement, even shortly afterwards. Before I pick up my dew-dampened table to leave, a kindly Plymouth Devils fan stops me, keen to say, "I really must apologise. This sort of stuff doesn't go on here usually!"

18th September 2010 Plymouth v. Weymouth (National Trophy) 48-44

Chapter Five – Rye House

The end of the world forecast is for 6pm. Everyone copes in their own way. Going towards Brighton is a red van sprayed with the words 'Pussy Wagon'. Judged by the look, décor and age of the vehicle rather than the signage, the driver is an optimist. In a hot, dusty Hoddesdon car park, the Rye House fans already there wait patiently with clipboards, fold-up chairs, flasks and sandwiches in preparation for Rye House 'Silver Ski' Rockets versus Somerset 'Dickies' Rebels rather than the forecast Rapture. With bright sunshine, light breeze and a cloudless sky – unless the world ends, the meeting will go ahead. With the turnstiles yet to open, Gaz can safely desert his race-day refreshment kiosk duties, "Oh God! He's here again! Watch it – he'll write down everything you say. Am I innit?"

[Jeff] "Yes."

[Gaz] "Saying what?"

[Jeff] "What you said."

[Gaz] "What, that you're a tosser?"

A tall tanned speedway rider with an Australian accent takes a close look at my display table, "Are they speedway books?"

[Jeff] "Yeh."

[speedway rider] "You write them?"

[Jeff] "Yeh."

[speedway rider] "Ah, cool!"

Andy Griggs's trackshop helper sees retro echoes in the young Australian's fashion sense, "Nelson is gonna get the shades to really look like Andrew Silver! He's already got the kevlars tucked in his boots."

Sam Masters and trackshop franchisee Andy Griggs chat animatedly about future merchandising plans, while the tall tanned young Tyson Nelson – Rye House Rockets reserve rider on an assessed 5 point average – waits. From the programme racecard, it's clear he's dropped his first name and prefers to be called Nelson. Promoter Len Silver's expresses surprise about other matters in his column (Len's Lines), "Nelson is struggling to find an engine that suits his style of riding". The recent away meeting at Newcastle saw both Luke Bowen and Steve Boxall return to the team. Apparently, Steve's return in place of Jason Frampton prompted ill-informed speculation on the speedway forums. Len sets the record straight, "A few people need to learn the FACTS about Steve's re-entry into the team. At the beginning of the season Steve was listed and registered for the Rockets. I had been totally satisfied that he was very fit and determined to do well and with good machinery to ride. Then he suffered that arm injury and other complications, which stopped him from riding. So I was lucky enough to sign Jason who was out of work at the time (though not for long as Poole needed him just a day or two later). The deal with Poole, Jason and the BSPA was that Jason would be a Rocket for as long as Steve was out of action, but that switch had to be reversed as soon as that situation changed. So for those few who thought I could keep both riders, it can be seen that this was not possible."

Discarded cotton wool flutters in the air and drifts into small piles against the concrete wall adjacent to the sand-covered ex-dog track that separates us from the speedway track. The raffle lady Shelly, explains, "It's the willows, they're all on this side of the river. We've had it for about three weeks now, it's nearly over. It's like cotton wool or snow, dry snow". The turnstiles open at 5pm, "You get a rush of the normals – all the people who travel a distance who like to come in straight away and then the real rush starts at 6.15pm until about quarter to seven." After the initial influx with the turnstiles temporarily becalmed, I go over to take photos.

[Michelle] "Why do you want to take our photos?"

[Irene] "Is it for the *Speedway Star*?"

[Michelle] "Is it because we're the friendliest?"

[Jeff] "Yes."

[Michelle] "We are. It's better to be that way. You get the best out of people, there's no point being otherwise."

[Jeff] "There's a nice breeze."

[Michelle] "There is. Usually it's freezing cold but, today, it's alright."

[Irene] "It's blowing in all the bits."

[Michelle] "You're lucky you've come now while it's earlier. We complain about it, whatever it is! Either it's too hot, too cold, or too windy. If you come back at quarter to seven, when it's really busy, you can hear all about it."

Passing the raffle stall, I overhear, "He's got the physique of a body builder!" As if on cue, Craig 'Mr Potassium' Saul arrives clutching two bananas, "I've got them specially for you." Craig's son Dan denies this claim, "You bring them every week." Craig puts his fruit to use. "When I arrived at Peterborough last week, I had one banana with me and I'd left the other in the car. Peter Oakes rushed up and said, 'Linus Sundström needs a banana for his pre-meeting meal.'"

[Jeff] "Why didn't he have one with him if it's his pre-meeting meal?"

[Craig] "I dunno! A lot of them have something greasy or drink a can of Red Bull. Later at heat 10, I said to him, 'There's no such thing as a free banana! You have to do an interview.' He was fine about it."

Only out a few days, Craig's already read quite a few chapters of my new book for interest and research. "I must get a second copy. I keep the other at home for best and travel with the other or lend it to people – so I know it'll come back dog-eared. Now that I'm at Lakeside, I get to see Scary Sheila la Sage every week. I didn't know about her until I read your books. When they said 'Scary' over the speakers until then I thought it was a name that shouldn't be mentioned. I also see Wendy – Miss Fina Invader – at Peterborough."

[Jeff] "Ah! Wendy Jedrzejakski."

Ever professional and alive to the nuances of pronunciation, Craig says, "Is that how you say it?"

[Jeff] "It's how I say it."

[Craig] "They must have shut in 1997 or 1998."

[Jeff] "I'm too polite to mention that, you can!"

Somerset programme editor, press officer and webmaster Ian Belcher temporarily leaves the pits. "It's our twelfth official meeting tonight and we've only fielded our top seven twice! That was during our first meeting of the season – even then Jimmy Holder crashed on his first ride on the third bend in heat 2 – and on Sunday, at home. We're lucky with Travis – he's got a high average – so we can have a guest because he's number 1. Dakota's will go up shortly. Rolling averages will work if they keep the system going."

[Jeff] "They'll abandon it in the winter."

[Ian] "Or sooner."

[Jeff] "Are you going in to win tonight?"

[Ian] "Depends which Rye House team turns up! The one that beat Ipswich or the one that lost to Newport at home! We'll do alright if Ty Proctor turns up! It's quarter to six and he's not here yet!"

[Jeff] "Are you going to all the meetings again this year?"

[Ian] "I'm not – I'm going away – missing eight matches."

[Jeff] "Eight!"

[Ian] "Yeh, it's best to take the other half away. We waited and waited and then booked a holiday in France. We both like the area where we're going – it's the Loire Valley – and can take the dog. Typically they don't publish the fixture lists and lots of meetings are on then – including the Scottish tour! I'm going to do a programme before I go and update the website while I'm away."

Like many Premier League fans, Ian struggles with the concept of the new 2011 structure. "The second half of the season is all wrong! You could end up with a situation where Glasgow gets Leicester, Somerset, Plymouth and Newport so they lose all the local derbies and get all the travel costs. Whereas, if at the start of the season, when all the teams are supposedly equal, they could split it into North and South, so you have all the local derbies at the start of the season and then again in the second half. They would also be able to publish the fixture list, which we don't know yet."

[Jeff] "Isn't it first, third, fifth?"

[Ian] "Nah, it's not odds and evens, it's more random than that! If you look at our website – Andy Povey does it – it has a breakdown. I know it goes second, fourth, fifth – that's the first bit anyway."

[Jeff] "Do you reckon you'll beat Leicester?"

[Ian] "When you come next week we'll have a bit of a Select side because Dakota North and Sam Masters will be away at the Under 21s and, hopefully, Travis will be back, we'll have a guest and Christian Hefenbrock or, maybe, not!"

With some gusto a familiar faced man bounds up. After friendly hellos he says, "You don't know who I am, do you? You usually see me at Sittingbourne. I must apologise for last year because, when I read the book, you had put in nice things about me. Sorry I doubted that! In addition to doing the reffing there, I sponsor the Amateur and Southern rider meetings. I'm the MTD Group – not many people know that or notice my number plate – JS5 MTD which gives it away!"

[Jeff] "No one is that observant."

[John Strong] "I'd rather sponsor the Amateur meetings where what I do makes a difference rather than do something elsewhere, which would be a drop in the bucket. I'm the incident recorder here, which I enjoy too!"

Craig Saul's dulcet tones burst loudly over the stadium speaker system, "A very sad Sunday – whoa – I'll put my teeth back in and start again, a very sunny and happy Saturday!" Craig bigs up the meeting ahead, name-checks all the facilities on offer inside Hoddesdon Stadium including the bar, acclaimed fish and chips as well as the trackshop ("all your Rye goodies from posters to pens and clothes"). Two smartly dressed women rush up with an urgent question, "Excuse me! It's our first time, can you bet on the races like the dogs?"

[Jeff] "No, you can't."

[Lady] "It would be good if you could and a good way of making some money!"

[Jeff] "You could bet among yourselves."

Reading speedway historian Arnie Gibbons is a man you can rely on for (questions and) answers. Is the predicted end of the world Rapture at 18.00 hours East Coast or West Coast time? "No, it's 6 o'clock local time. I was listening to Radio 2 on the way here and, when there was the handover, Alan Carr said, 'I haven't got anything prepared for the show!'" Arnie's History of the Reading Racers is a critical and sales success, "When I closed the accounts on my book it had made a profit, which I've used – in part – to sponsor Phil Morris's testimonial in September and the Under-19's trip to Sweden!"

With his presentational work still to properly get underway, Craig Saul listens to Arnie's forthcoming concert plans, "I'm going to see John Cooper Clarke and John Otway at the Royal Festival Hall. The last time I saw John Otway was at the Lucas Aerospace Sports and Social Club in Hemel Hempstead!" Music at speedway meetings is variable. Arnie's international travel takes him to obscure places, "The worst evening's music at speedway ever was over at Grindsted (in Denmark). They played Smokey's greatest hits and, when they finished, they played it again!" I like to hear about embarrassing gigs. Craig confesses, "I went to see Can play at Bournemouth Winter Gardens. There were 25 people in the audience only and that was embarrassing – they came on 40 minutes late." Arnie recalls, "As I'm Reading born and bred, I went to the Reading Festival and saw Wayne County and the Electric Chairs. This was before he became Jayne. They sang two songs, '(You Make Me) Cream in my Jeans' and 'Fuck Off', I think, before a hail of cans drove them from the stage."

[Craig] "At the last night of the season at Peterborough in 1993, Rod Colhoun had been dropped from the team and he brought his guitar along and played it in the bar. He played a spoof of 'Knocking on Heaven's Door' called 'Knocking on Kevin's Door'."

[Arnie] "You don't want to be standing next to [toe sucker] David Mellor at the Royal Opera House urinals. Your mind turns to things you don't want to contemplate! The timings work very well of Glyndebourne and Eastbourne speedway together! It starts an hour or two before the speedway and finishes at almost the same time. So I can drop my husband off on the way there and pick him up on the way back."

Craig's duties call him away. Arnie's got no sympathy with people who doubt the legitimacy of Peter Adams's recent double use of tactical rides as rider replacement. "The rules over using tactical rides in a rider replacement are perfectly clear. As the brains trust on the British Speedway Forum points out, it's not ruled out, so it is legal! A better question is, as a guest is only allowed for a number 1 or a British entrant in the Under 21s, so how did Leicester get a guest for Richard Sweetman a few weeks ago when they should have had rider replacement?" Arnie's joy at the return of Leicester is unalloyed. "It's only 80 minutes to Rye House from my house and 2 hours 5 minutes to Leicester. Going back is all about reliving my glory days. I'm standing there chatting with people I stood with 28 years ago! When you go, watch out for people with Ray Wilson rosettes. Apart from the fact the racing has been a bit disappointing because the tracks been a bit hit and miss, I think the problem – and I'm not an expert – has been the extraordinarily dry weather, which has made the track like concrete with a shale top surface. If you water it now, it's concrete and it runs off. Most people have been tolerant and understanding. At least they avoided the Wimbledon problem of a first meeting of sludge. The other thing is the announcer. It will disappoint you to hear that he probably won't be there when you go for the Berwick meeting. He's been announcing race results in random order. Fourth places and a 4-1. Telling us who was fourth was one thing but he also had a tendency to announce riders not there and to forget programme changes. Promoter David Hemsley has the cycle speedway connection so they're getting in the cycle person. I went to the first away meeting and that was really moving! I went to the first practice meeting and that was extraordinarily uplifting! There were all those people I used to stand with or know. The last time I saw Keith was at your table in Peterborough in 2006. He goes with his dad who's in his 80s. And there's Elmo who was an impressionable 16-year old when Leicester packed up in 1983, now he's a parent and I have to think of my language!" Arnie isn't fussed with the furore over the new silencers, "I must admit I only notice it if I consciously listen! It must be an extension of being tone deaf."

Veteran speedway promoter and inveterate showman, Len Silver takes to the microphone. "Welcome to our good friends from Somerset and the people from Somerset – hello my dears, hope you enjoy the meeting." After various further greetings and comment, Len soon gets down to rider introductions. "They've not got their ginger-haired Australian [Travis McGowan] instead they've got a very clever guest from Wolverhampton – and the Wolverhampton track is almost identical to ours – Ty Proctor. Dakota North – their number 2 – has made a difference with a surge of form showing that he's a champion. Christian Hefenbrook – he's the German who's broken his ribs so they run rider replacement. Sam Masters – a rider who loves our track. Cory Gathercole – another Aussie: they do love them from Down Under! Alex Davies – I think they got that one just past the BSPA – and James Holder, we saw him here for Ipswich".

Len continues with his own team, "Number 1 as always, Jordan Frampton!" Arnie interjects, "It's not always – it was Jason Doyle!" Echoing his programme notes, Len welcomes back Luke Bowen, Ritchie Hawkins ("getting better week by week"), Chris Neath, ("Mr Rye House"), "Let's give a big welcome back to the team for Steve Boxall [big cheer] and let's also welcome our reserves: Ben Morley and Nelson." Arnie tuts, "I do hate this affectation – his name is Tyson Nelson!" After the formality of the toss for gate positions between captains James Holder and Chris Neath, Len traditionally throws the "lucky £2 coin" to the gaggle of youngsters who gather by the start line for this very purpose ("not much blood tonight – shame!") Arnie sighs, "I get the impression that the locals do not regard Steve Boxall for Jason Doyle as strengthening the team!"

After an amendment to our programmes ("there's one typo in heat 2 – Chris Neath isn't riding, it's Ben Morley"), Craig Saul gives a warm Rye House shout-out welcome, "to the Royal Mail and the Hertfordshire Constabulary who are guests in the hospitality suite tonight!" After a drawn heat 1, Craig completes his race line-up introduction for the next race with, "The sheer guts and explosive excitement – yes, yes, it's Nelson!" The race fails to get meaningfully underway because James Holder demolishes the tapes, "there's movement at the line there – there's disqualification for James Holder – a visitor here with Ipswich recently – for finding, nay breaking, the tapes there!" In the rerun, Rebels reserve Alex Davies completes a comfortable victory to admiration from Craig, "making a very promising debut there – Alex Davies with a time of 57.9 second for the 18-year old." Effortlessly knowledgeable, Craig tops and tails each race with facts, insight and information in an unobtrusive but useful fashion. Chris Neath takes Sam Masters right out for a close inspection of the third bend fence before he zooms away. "I tell you Chris looked fast in that one! He wasn't fast enough to beat his own track record of 55.1 seconds, but he was fast at 55.6 seconds".

Judged by the racecard, heat 4 pits Steve Boxall ("it's our first look at the rider in red. A re-debut, if you can call it that, after that meeting at Newcastle") against Cory Gathercole ("a third year Rebel after two seasons on the Isle of Wight"). The reality is different since Boxall and Nelson hammer home ahead of James Holder. "Winning on his debut again, I give you the Boxmeister – Steve Boxall!" This is a win greeted ecstatically by a small knot of Steve Boxall's family and friends gathered on the steps outside the bar. Steve Boxall's mum asks the young boy next to her, "Do you like it then?" He does! Plus he's got some good advice of his own, "Always red or blue, always!" The advice blows freely, "I tell him: everyone else don't care about your teammates! They're professionals, they can look out for themselves." Gaz warns another unsuspecting fan, "Don't stand here, he'll be writing every blooming thing down. He is a flapper-jacker!" Heats 5 and 6 are drawn after reruns. Luke Bowen's falls and disqualification from heat 6 sees him take no further part in the meeting.

The night suddenly takes a possibly promising turn when Hester Adams asks, "Are you Jeff Scott? I came tonight because I saw you were to be here on your website. I came here specifically to see you! The website said you'd be here. Dunno how I got there? I brought my son Eddie – it's a break from his GCSEs – he's over there. I think he's quite enjoying it." Away from the track Hester is a councillor. She also freelances as a television researcher, hence her trip to Rye House speedway tonight. However, from the scant details I gather about the programme Hester researches, it's a reasonable assumption that someone at the television company reads the local newspaper reports. "Someone had an idea in the bath and thought speedway would be a great setting for a Channel 4 crime programme! It's nothing more than an idea at the moment. I can tell you no more than that, but I wondered if I could ask you some questions?" For the next six or so heats – between the race action and my vital programme work – Hester quizzes me and takes copious notes.

Though speedway can shoot itself in the foot, Hester soon learns we keep our real/imaginary dirty washing within the strict confines of the immediate speedway family.

Similarly, no matter how many times I press Hester for further detail about the conceptualisation and/or draft storylines of this series idea, it's clear that though she has questions to ask, she's only prepared to let minimal details leak out about the tentative project she researches. Taking my cue from James Bond films, I volunteer to eat any evidence, "If I tell you any more then I'll have to shoot you". That said, without previous experience of speedway, Hester implicitly reveals – through her thumbnail sketches of the cardboard cut-out story arcs and the (cartoon-like) characters – the lowly status speedway must hold in the vivid imaginations of the editors and writers for this prospective unnamed Channel 4 crime programme strand. Questions Hester asks include:

Could someone disappear into the speedway community?

Where do they live?

What cars do they drive?

How does the community react to outsiders?

How does the community react to unusual behaviour?

Is speedway a full-time job?

What else do they do?

From what you're saying, they travel huge distances and, sometimes, they sleep in their vans – how can they afford to do that?

What does it cost to be a speedway rider?

Are there many disputes?

Serious disputes?

What do they get paid?

What do you think is the attitude towards the police?

And rules?

How do disputes get resolved?

Is there a drink or drugs problem?

Groupies?

What age are they?

Where do they come from?

What would they do if they weren't speedway riders?

Does the community sort out any problems itself or does it involve outside bodies like the police?

Are many riders vegetarians?

Hester asks way too many questions. It's quickly apparent my books don't contain enough salacious information. Though sadly they're not on sale in Andy Griggs's trackshop, I tell Hester for further research into shadier goings on in the speedway world, then almost any issue of *Backtrack* has something. Or, if she seeks real life stories of fights, lawlessness, match fixing, drugs, groupies and general shenanigans, then Tony MacDonald publishes a whole raft of ex-rider autobiographies in his Retro Speedway imprint. Presently stood in a world she wouldn't usually expect to enjoy, Hester's keen to offer reassurance. "I'm a researcher, I was only told yesterday. I might be in touch again, it depends how they want to flesh out the characters or develop them with this and the other information I find out. I really don't know." Hester reconfirms that my books are, effectively, pretty sanitised, "That's very unusual to send your chapters to people before you publish! I suppose you are part of the community and want to remain so." Earlier, Hester moseyed around the stadium, "They make a big thing out of the VIP area but it's only a little square!" Nonetheless, her son Eddie likes the speed, flamboyance and competitiveness of riders' racing and is surprised by their matter-of-fact reaction to crashes. "This is much better than Formula 1!"

With all the questions, it's been hard to concentrate on the meeting. After seven drawn heats (out of eight) consecutive Rockets 4-2s follow. Steve Boxall wins heat 11 and gains praise from Craig Saul, "He gives 110% effort. He's got so much potential but sometimes it doesn't go as well as he'd like." Heat 12 sees a win for Nelson, while the next race takes three attempts to run. Nine points up with two races to go requires Craig Saul to outline the permutations, "Should Rye House produce finishers in heats 14 and 15, they should win the match! The Rebels still have that outside shout". With Chris Neath first and Nelson third in the penultimate race, Rye effectively seal the deal. Ultra-professionally, Craig remains wary, "barring the catastrophe of a 5-0 that's a [3 point] win for Rye House!" Captain Chris Neath celebrates his race win with vigour, "To paraphrase the song – Don't Stop Me Now! Chris Neath is having a fine time out there on the track." Neath's enthusiasm and good form continues into the last race where he follows Jordan Frampton. "We've had many drawn results this evening and only three maximums, and one of them comes in the last race of the evening!" Celebrations continue but Craig remembers the casualties ("A Get Well message for Luke Bowen"). For Arnie, Somerset fail to show the resistance anticipated, "They weren't very rebellious!" Returnee speedway fan Dexter says, "It's the first time I've been in 25 years. I came here and Hackney from 77-85. It's changed a bit but it's great to be back!"

En route for the car park (and, possibly, more bananas), Craig Saul puts me right on my claim, "Len is doing a Jon Cook with the introductions on parade." "No Jon Cook is doing a Len!! Len's been doing it for years. You should hear Jon Cook he's phenomenal. Before I heard him I thought 'I know it could be Jon Cook's ego run wild' but he was amazing! It's all in his head without notes: just looking down the line of riders. Obviously, he knows his own but he knew all the Poole riders too. He gives the fans insight and insider knowledge – all without notes! I love working with someone who speaks his mind. You don't know what he'll say and that means everyone really listens. Stuart [Douglas] writes well and is a good guy. There are lots of really great people at Lakeside. I've been announced as the new announcer – though I tell Jon Cook I live two hours away so can't always get to them all – but he asked me to do the Test and Birmingham. He's so easy to work with. I enjoy the interviews. Robbo's only 34. I know I always think of him as an old fellow – he's handy on the mic and good to work with too. Troy is my 'go to interviewee' at Peterborough. He's got so much talent and he's really professional and focused this season!"

21st May Rye House v. Somerset 2011 (Premier League) 54-39

Chapter Six – Wolverhampton

....

I dash from the Hoddesdon circuit to my car before the protracted Rye House meeting is over because I worry it could be a long and congested 145 mile drive in the Bank Holiday traffic from Hertfordshire to the Black Country and the Monmore Green Stadium. It's the self-styled "Theatre of Thrills" and home of the Parry's International Wolves. I don't want to be late for my appointment to meet the hugely experienced Peter Adams, who wears many hats at the club in his roles as co-promoter, speedway manager and team manager. I will also meet Chris van Straaten with whom I'd discussed my visit a few days previously. He is another of the long-serving speedway stalwarts that comprise the club's triumvirate of co-promoters and, until recently, was the chairman of the sport's governing body, the BSPA. From my call, I understand that they've both agreed to meet with me to briefly discuss all things speedway and Wolverhampton Speedway in particular for my book. That is if I get there early, a few hours before the Bank Holiday evening Elite League 'A' fixture against the Eastbourne Eagles.

To find the stadium is a fairly straightforward task if you follow the glamorously named Black Country Route from the motorway, which is in fact the A454. It is very well signposted to the stadium in Sutherland Avenue, an area that is a strange mix of reasonably attractive parkland combined with a number of light industrial buildings. I arrive early. The substantial gates to the stadium car park remain forbiddingly shut and the huge expanse of empty car park looks particularly desolate. There appears to be very little sign of life, it's eerily silent, but then it is a Bank Holiday. I buzz the intercom, explain myself and the gates very slowly swing open to allow me into the vast car park. I'm followed by another car full of fans that have also arrived very early for this meeting. Since I have a wide choice of parking spaces, I park very close to the shuttered turnstile entrance to the stadium, which announces itself as 'Ladbrokes Stadium Monmore' in large letters on the side of its roof. The entry prices appear to be exceptionally good value for the Elite League, especially the charge of £7 for the so-called 'concession' fans – mostly the unemployed, students and old age pensioners – of whom the latter still resolutely remain the most important, loyal and largest demographic group at most speedway tracks. I've wanted to visit the Wolverhampton track for many years. They always seem to have a substantial number of fanatical fans, dressed in the team colours or other old gold and black coloured branded items of clothing, who travel to loudly support their team whenever they ride at Eastbourne. I'd also heard stories of massive crowds, informed fans and a generally fantastic atmosphere at Monmore Green Stadium from Kevin Donovan, the man who I'd used to stand next to at Arlington. He'd taken his girlfriend to watch them ride against Eastbourne, a trip that had the added bonus and attraction of a rather wild Nicki Pedersen who then rode for the Wolves. Nicki had attracted everyone's attention earlier in the season with a hard riding but thrilling display of riding at Arlington – where he easily gained the mantle of the visiting rider that everyone loved to hate, mostly because of his ability, skill and obvious aggression. The visit to Monmore hadn't been great, if you were an Eastbourne fan, but for weeks afterwards Kevin waxed lyrical about how extremely passionate, friendly and knowledgeable the Wolves' fans were about the sport and their team. The general interest was so intense that he'd been amazed to find "even the birds are really mad for it up there!"

The mobility of speedway riders in general and the top riders of this contemporary generation in particular is remarkable. In the Elite League the process is especially pronounced and, to be fair, often exaggerated by team changes caused by injuries to riders. However, loyalty from promoters towards the riders has dwindled as well. While the reality of the situation is that all riders are self-employed and have to constantly seek the best deal for themselves each season; this leaves the loyal fans of any one club to often bemoan the whirlwind of rider changes within their team during the season as well as from year to year. The situation is further complicated by the ownership rules that apply to the rider's individual contracts. These contracts often remain the property of a promoter or ex-promoter for whose team the rider no longer appears, but for whom they still receive a loan fee when the rider appears for another club. It's not the type of restrictive contractual situation that would apply to ordinary jobs, under current UK and European employment law, let alone in other sports. It would be unimaginable in football, for example, where such practices would cause a national furore in the press and on television. But this is speedway and different ways of business often appear to apply and will continue to do so until challenged or, most likely, until it suits the contract owners themselves to change.[1]

Unusually, Eastbourne have a reputation within the sport, over the last few years, for consistency and loyalty in their choice of team personnel and, compared to most other clubs in their League, they are a model of constancy with their staff. However, the nature of the speedway beast inevitably forces some changes to team line ups and, as a result, this now finds Nicki Pedersen as Eastbourne's top rider since he joined the club in mid 2003, the year he became World Champion. His own journey around the Elite League clubs in this country illustrates my point because since he left the Wolves, after the completion of the 2000 season, he has then travelled via King's Lynn and Oxford to end up at the Eagles. This has catapulted him from a heroic figure status always lauded by the Wolverhampton faithful to his present pariah status of 'Public Enemy Number 1'. Many of the Eastbourne fans have had a similar emotional journey with Nicki (but in the opposite direction from that experienced

[1] at some future point speedway contracts will definitely undergo their own re-evaluation and revision, equivalent to the revolutionary impact of the Bosman ruling in football, but only after the contractual situation is legally challenged by a brave and suitably disgruntled rider.

by the previously adoring Wolves' crowd) who now inspires great loyalty and devotion from the Arlington faithful in equal measure to the previous opprobrium. Within the sport, Nicki Pedersen is arguably the most controversial current rider who presently works in the sport, often seen to be as popular as a rattlesnake in a lucky dip by the fans of rival teams, and there is a highly critical opinion about his reputation for hard riding that means he's invariably portrayed as a villain. Only marginally more popular than Danish cartoonists to Muslims and just as often disparaged, off the track Nicki can be charming, diffident and gentle. But once that crash helmet is on and he's racing on the track, he competes to win at all costs. From a fan's perspective, the races he's involved in will always be exciting and often controversial because of his 'hard riding' style. However, as they say that the definition of an alcoholic is someone who drinks the same as you do, but is someone you don't like, so similarly, the definition of a hard or unfair rider would be someone who's just as aggressive as your team's riders, but who rides for another team.

Whatever your opinion, it certainly makes very good box office and speedway as a sport is usually keen to stress the thrill and entertainment that the racing often provides. Nonetheless, I expect the partisan Wolverhampton crowd will be even more vociferous and pumped up for this evening's encounter. As I walk through the open gates by the shuttered turnstiles, the noticeable silence is broken only by the sound of the tractor that repeatedly pulls the bowser round the circuit to intensively water the track. The tractor is painted in the old gold and black of the home team and the bowser is similarly coloured with the logo 'Wolverhampton Speedway' painted in black letters on its side. Although it's a bright, sunny afternoon, rain is forecast later and it's noticeable that there are already a few rain clouds that have begun to threaten on the horizon. I'm so early that Chris van Straaten hasn't yet arrived at the track, so I take the chance to explore the large modern home-straight grandstand. I walk up the airy stairwell to look at the track from the first floor of the grandstand. There's also a large bar and refreshment area, though it's presently closed as the stadium's entrance gates have yet to open, though some of the staff have sat down to have a chat and a hot drink together before their preparations for the evening's work begin. The refreshment area itself appears to stretch the length of the home straight and provides an excellent view of the whole circuit, which comprises of greyhound and speedway tracks, through the large glass windows. The grandstands in modern greyhound stadiums definitely cater to their punters who want to be able to uninterruptedly watch the evening's racing without the need to venture outside or even leave their seat, except maybe to get some refreshments or to use the adjacent facilities. The dog track itself is covered with tarpaulin held down with tyres to prevent shale polluting the racing surface. Quite a large area of the perimeter of the stadium fence is thickly lined with trees, especially on the back straight, and their height indicates that they've been around for some while. This gives the whole stadium environment an unexpectedly rural feel and it contradicts the preconceived image that the mention of Wolverhampton usually conjures in your mind. This impression even applies to the pits area, which lies adjacent to some low-roofed office buildings, since it boasts a large grassy area sandwiched between the pits and the fence that guards bends 1 and 2 of the dog and speedway tracks. Both sides of the pits areas have grey-roofed open-fronted sheds in front of a line of tall trees. The final element of this more rural effect is the route from the pits to the track itself that passes behind a large tree hedge that wouldn't look out of place in a suburban garden but seems slightly incongruous at a speedway track. Later, I notice that some of the riders make quick use of its screening effect.

There's a flat-roofed building next to the pits, which I'm told is where I should find both Chris van Straaten and Peter Adams. When I get there it turns out they have finally arrived, but are locked in together in earnest discussion about something urgent that's just come up and that definitely won't permit Chris to speak with me. Though when reminded, he appears to have completely forgotten my call and our subsequent arrangement. I do, however, learn that in quarter of an hour or so Peter will kindly have a few minutes available to chat over a coffee on the benches near to the office. In the meantime, I head over to the Wolves' track shop, which is located by the grandstand in an ideal position for people who pass by either towards the pits or to stand on the open, tiered terraces in front of the grandstand. When you watch on television, this part of the stadium is always absolutely packed with loudly enthusiastic fans, as you imagine the rest of the stadium is at any Wolves' speedway fixture. However, this impression depends on an optical illusion, because when I look around it soon becomes clear that this appears to be the only place you can actually stand within the stadium to watch the action on the track. This, perhaps, makes sense since the stadium is primarily used as a dog track and so this is where the key action will always happen. Though the atmosphere is better with the crowd all packed together and it enhances the notorious Black Country camaraderie, it's not always been like this. The old stadium used to wrap round the third and fourth bends, with a covered stand on the back straight; indeed, many local fans jokingly call it the slowly disappearing stadium as the number of places to stand has gradually shrunk.

The avuncular and helpful Dave Rattenberry owns the track shop. He sets out the vast array of stock on the tables he has arranged for this purpose with his capable assistant, John Rich, under the temporary stand they construct each week and then cover with tarpaulin. From the impressive piles of coloured boxes and containers they have already unloaded, the set out an attractive display of every conceivable type of speedway accoutrement or memorabilia imaginable. There's a huge range of Wolverhampton merchandise with a great emphasis upon upper body clothing in a wide variety of sizes, particularly for the larger framed fan. There are anoraks, "hoodies" as the government has now taught us we should call them, sweatshirt tops and T-shirts that completely line the back wall of their shop area. The tables heave with old programmes, badges, pens, rider and team photographs, programme boards, some quite cute teddies and all the usual accessories, inevitably covered in the Wolverhampton or Wolves' logo. These include air horns since these can be used without limit at Monmore Green Stadium because there is no curfew and no near neighbours to bother with noise disturbance. I glance through some of the old programmes and the recent magazines, and take the chance to point out a photo from 1974 that I'd previously noticed in the latest edition of *Backtrack*[2], which features a very youthful looking Chris van Straaten when he was team manager of Stoke. We chortle at how long and almost hippyish his hair looks before Dave and John rather seriously remind me that that sort of unkempt look was ubiquitous but still seen as fashionable back then.

Along with all the clothes that line the back tarpaulin wall is a bookstand that displays many recently published books. Dave believes that there are too many books published nowadays, especially ghost written or collaborative 'autobiographies' of famous riders, and some biographies, which often don't sell that well at the tracks where they riders hadn't regularly ridden. Uncontroversially, the best seller at Monmore is a history of the club written by Mark Sawbridge who has "phenomenal knowledge and is a very nice lad". Dave wishes me well with my book of my travels throughout the country and claims that it should have some appeal to the network of track-shop franchises that he runs around the country. He used to run more than he does nowadays but there was a falling out with Oxford and "that Wagstaff" over money. Money was the root of all evil at Coventry as well, although Dave notes that they additionally cover you in ordure at Brandon. That still leaves him a healthy network of shops that includes Buxton and Stoke. It must quite some business, or, at least, one Dave Rattenberry is very proud to manage if John Rich's blue shirt is anything to judge by. It has a prominent multi-coloured stitched logo of a rampant rider broad siding, surrounded by a circle of letters. The top half proclaims in white stitched letters 'DR Promotional Leisurewear' while yellow stitching at the bottom notes the unusual combination of 'Embroidery and Track Shops'. Like so many others with any connection to any club on race day, they're both huge fans of speedway that sincerely appreciate the great support of the fans traditionally given at the Wolves to go along with the excellence of the race track that they usually prepare at Monmore. They're also keen to

[2] the always captivating retro speedway magazine covers the speedway era from 1970s to 1990, and is published by the enterprising Tony McDonald

sing the praises of the consistently high quality meetings you witness at the Stoke and Somerset racetracks, which they predict I'll enjoy when I visit.

The shop appears to act as a magnet for everyone who arrives at the stadium. The announcer Shaun Leigh stops by for a few words before he leaves for the commentary box to conduct some vital technical checks and preparations. He also has his own regular circuit of clubs where he works as announcer every week. These tracks are located in the Yorkshire–Lincolnshire triangle of Hull, Scunthorpe and include Sheffield, where he also does the stock cars, which is particularly handy as he lives only a quarter of a mile away from the stadium. On an afternoon in praise of good quality speedway entertainment, Shaun singles out the country's newest track Scunthorpe, located "in the middle of a field", and the "very nice" promoters there, Rob and Norman. The referee for tonight's fixture, Chris Durno, echoes this opinion and describes it as a "great set up; anything you want them to do, they do". He has also been drawn to the shop, via the speedway office, where he has learnt some dramatic news. Everyone then has what could best be described as an old wives' meeting, with lots of oohs and ums, as they discuss the news that Wolves will ride tonight without their Number 1 rider Michael Max and his younger brother Magnus Karlsson since they both remain stranded in Sweden. They have different surnames because, a few years ago, after Michael had rode for many years as a 'Karlsson', he then decided to revert to his mother's maiden name of Max, ostensibly, but somewhat mysteriously, to try to distinguish himself from his speedway racing brothers Peter and Magnus. There's unanimity at the shop that this state of affairs is precisely the logical consequence and peril that modern promoters inevitably run when they rely so heavily on so many foreign-based riders within their team. The exact circumstances of their non-appearance haven't been exactly or satisfactorily established, but they all have been told the same story, albeit until now ano one has yet shared it with me. It appears that the brothers returned to Sweden, in order to enjoy a rare long weekend, but failed to allow for unforeseen events when they decided to schedule their return on a Monday, the day of their next Wolves' meeting, rather than more sensibly to return on a Sunday flight. Unfortunately for them and the Wolves' fans, their plane had developed unexpected 'technical problems' so, despite having cleared customs and immigration control, they were left without sufficient time to find an alternative route after their flight was then cancelled. This leaves the Wolves' promotion, management and team well and truly up a gum tree and faced with the prospect of competing with a massively depleted team for this evening's fixture with Eastbourne. Since they drew the away leg of the equivalent fixture at Arlington, where I believe they were maybe unlucky not to actually win, they would have had understandably high hopes of a home victory that would also secure the additional bonus point. These would be vital points, even at this early stage of the season, particularly as they would follow on from a few away defeats and the embarrassment of an Elite League home loss to Belle Vue. The bumper Bank Holiday crowd of fans due to arrive through the stadium gates in a few minutes will definitely be quite right to feel short changed and cheated with a home team line up deprived of these key riders.

No wonder, Chris and Peter were locked in an important meeting in the office and suddenly unable to see me earlier. A few minutes later I do get to sit down with Peter who still takes the time to have a coffee and a chat despite all that's happened. If the truth were told, he appears distracted and harassed as well as a little wary of my intentions. We chat about my research and travel plans before I produce my list of prepared questions that I'd like to ask him. Peter honestly states straightaway, "I don't like answering questions off the cuff". He'd much prefer to consider them before he answers, then chat on the phone another time or meet up before the next Wolves' fixture at Arlington later in the year. He's totally reluctant to talk about the missing riders, his thoughts on their absence and what he intends to do this evening before he soon heads back to the speedway office. It's a shame we can't talk, especially as Peter is one of the people I'd most looked forward to a talk with on my travels. Particularly because he always appears so thoughtful and analytical, albeit slightly taciturn, when he appears on national television or commits his opinions to print.

Instead I decide to venture up to the referee's box, where Chris had invited me to consider the Monmore Green Stadium track from his perspective. When I arrive Shaun is in mid-fiddle with his announcer's equipment, while Chris has his blue SCB rulebook ostentaciously held open for a closer inspection of the relevant section that includes the exact regulations that apply to suddenly absent riders. He does this simultaneously while he conducts an animated and lengthy discussion on his mobile phone, about the various possible scenarios that apply to these unusual circumstances. Chris confirms what I had suspected, but that his guarded 'public' demeanour mostly disguised, that Peter Adams is "like a bear with a sore head" and was "absolutely scathing" about his missing team members. He's strongly suggested that the referee "report them to the SCB" and wants Chris to ensure that they "implement the maximum penalty fines allowable under the circumstances" at them. Chris explains that he's consulted with other referees on the notorious referees' grapevine, just to ensure that his interpretation of the rules with regard to substitute riders is correct. Every referee is agreed that since Max and Karlsson have been nominated in the Wolves' team already, then it's impossible at the last minute to replace the Number 1 rider Max with a guest or rider replacement. The Wolves have been left with little other available options but to replace Max with a young, promising but inexperienced Conference League rider from Stoke, Jack Hargreaves, and to replace Karlsson, who was programmed to ride at reserve, with locally based Tony Atkin, who literally dropped everything to answer the emergency call to shoot across to Monmore Green to fill in at the very last minute. This team line up will leave the home side severely depleted and leaves Adams "desperate for a thunderstorm to cancel this meeting". With the mention of rain, we both instinctively glance out at the tractor that still continues to intensively water the track with the bowser. Whatever happens, Chris notes with some understatement, "it's going to be interesting". Wolves will attempt to mitigate disappointment in the crowd by warning the fans of the late change to the team; both via the club call line and by posting information notices on the turnstiles.

However, the majority of fans will be already on their way to the stadium confident that the meeting will definitely be held on an intermittently sunny, fine but cloudy evening.

Chris takes some time to explain many of the details about the work of a qualified SCB referee. Like many people who work in speedway, their work is a labour of love that involves many hours of dedicated work with little financial reward. The officials are another vital part of the essential staff every track requires, the grassroots of the sport if you will, without which speedway in this country wouldn't be able to continue and function. Later I learn that the referees receive travel expenses and a small nominal payment for their work, although very different from the compulsory SCB fee of £100, in advance, for the services of their officials. Chris deliberately notes that, "so many people who do menial tasks at a speedway track do so without pay, usually because they're very passionate". He describes the lengthy qualification procedure that any would-be 'trainee' referees have to endure to become qualified and able to take charge of a meeting. This apprenticeship involves many hours of travel throughout the country at their own expense, while they shadow experienced qualified referees as well as undertaking rigorous study of the ever-changing rulebook. Ultimately, you get to take part in a qualifying sequence of three meetings that you referee under supervision. This effectively constitutes your pass-or-fail examination. Many people immediately drop out at the first hurdle when they learn about the long hours of travel and the wear and tear on their cars, and even then for those that manage to continue their apprenticeship the attrition rate is high. The attrition is due to the "ruthless and quite brutal" rigour of continual study allied to the stringent tests, which cause many of the trainees to "crash and burn". Out of the cohort of eleven trainees Chris started with, only four survived to qualify and it often comes down to the "survival of the fittest" and those adaptable enough to the "long hours, stress and loneliness". Each trainee referee adapts to the training programme in their own manner and takes a different length of time to serve their apprenticeship, usually a couple of years, before they pass. Chris passed in June 2002 and relishes his work as a referee. But the job makes huge demands on your family and spare time with many referees only able to do the job if they are self-employed or if they use all their holiday entitlement in order to fulfil their refereeing obligations. Chris suggests that at another meeting I join him for an entire evening to get a real insight into a job the fans, promoters and riders consistently underestimate and take for granted.[3]

The view from the referee's box is panoramic and, according to Chris, an ideal example of the type of facility you would want to work in as a referee – one in which you cannot be distracted by the crowd. At Wolves you're perched way above the heads of the fans and enjoy an uninterrupted view without the possibility of the supporters "getting stuck in" with their strongly felt opinions. However, unlike the other tracks Chris praises – Belle Vue, Coventry and Oxford – this box is disadvantaged not only by its small size, but it's also located 30 or so yards ahead of the start/finish line which can make those ragged starts and close finish decisions very difficult. This wasn't always such an insurmountable problem for disputed close finishes since you could always unofficially consult the "scrupulously fair line marshal for his second opinion in particularly close calls". Now, however, this is something that Chris van Straaten has the power to put a stop to, and, as a consequence, the referees now must make the final decision without the benefit of this different perspective.

Outside the gates have opened and there's already quite a crowd of people gathered round the track shop, on the nearby benches or who congregate in their favourite spot on the terraces. Many more of the fans have made their way to the pits area and are either in the pits to chat with the riders and mechanics, or else they linger on the grass and watch the activity. There's a much bigger crowd by the home pits area and many of the riders happily sign autographs or pose for photographs with the fans. Small but kindly gestures can make all the difference to your perceptions of a place. A cheery "how are ya?" in a broad Australian strine from Wolves' Captain Steve Johnson, directed to myself for no

---

[3] for alternative insight into the politics and the paperwork as well as the trials and tribulations involved to become a qualified SCB official, I'd recommend the self-published pamphlet *A Ref's Tale* by Dave Osborne.

reason other than to greet me as I pass him, makes me instantly feel right at home. I'm already feeling particularly privileged since I have been invited along as a guest of Jon Cook, Eastbourne's knowledgeable promoter. We'd chatted about my book and he felt that, with Chris van Straaten's permission, because of its unique layout Wolverhampton would be the ideal track to closely observe all that happens in the pits as well as on the track itself. I stroll over and let Jon know I've arrived. He doesn't feel well and wants the meeting to proceed, despite the threat of rain, as he'd rather not have to travel back to the Midlands again for a rescheduled meeting. We watch the intensive watering continue and he shrugs philosophically, "with the team they've got tonight, it's nothing more than we would do if it was at our place and we wanted to ensure it got abandoned if it rains". He explained where I could stand – just by the motorway-style sleeper dividers that separate the pits from the grass bank that leads to the track fences – once the pits had been cleared of the fans 30 minutes before the fixture starts. This would give me the ideal vantage point to follow exactly what happens on the Eastbourne side of the pits, or the Wolves' pits adjacent to it and, for the races themselves, I can easily wander across the grass bank to get to see. I'm delighted to be so close, if slightly in awe of the riders and mechanics who now busily prepare their bikes. I hesitate to interrupt them or Jon, particularly as he says, "right I'm off to do my job of managing".

Rather than intrude on the preparations I chat with the man beside me on the grass. Tony Charsley has travelled up from Stoke on public transport, as he does regularly, to watch the Wolves. He lives across the road from the Stoke track, which he notes has "brilliant racing but a crap stadium". He's been hooked on speedway ever since he went to his first meeting, New Cross versus Wimbledon in 1949, and feels that it's something that just gets into your blood. He's always admired the riders for not whinging when they fall, they "just get up and get on with it", unlike many other sports in his opinion, particularly football where he believes that they've become fitter not better. Tony has always had a penchant for stylish riders, especially Gordon Kennett, someone he thinks should have been World Champion. But then there have been so many riders with lots of skill and ability that never became the World Champions during the era they rode in. He wistfully and quickly reels off the names of Olly Nygren, Jack Parker, Brian Crutcher "who retired at 26", Chris Morton and the Moran brothers. His all-time favourite is Ronnie Moore, who was " a gentleman, did nothing dirty but lacked that killer instinct". Tony still loves the thrill of the racing and passing, even on modern tracks with modern equipment, though he thinks the tracks aren't as good as they once were because they lack "the dirt" of yesteryear. It's a problem both created and compounded by the present riders having highly tuned, powerful machines that "just don't like the dirt".

People still surround the riders and mechanics, who continue with their preparations, but still courteously find the time to pose for photos or sign autographs. Nicki Pedersen is extremely popular and is in huge demand but is also clearly very practised at public relations. As he kneels by a particularly recalcitrant and grumpy small boy who is very reluctant to pose for the photograph his father so obviously desires, Nicki gently but repeatedly pleads with him to "smile for Daddy". Eventually, the boy's resolve lightens at Nicki's gentle but persuasive persistence before father and son finally go off happily to the grandstand terraces.

At 7 p.m. sharp, the time has come for the riders, mechanics and team managers to concentrate on the Elite League fixture at hand. The pits area is cleared of all members of the public and I feel suitably privileged to stay to watch proceedings first hand. The only other person who remains but doesn't help in the Eastbourne side of the pits is an extremely tall man who turns out to be Dean Saunders, not the notorious footballer, but in fact the proud sponsor of Davey Watt via his construction company Saunders Surfacing Contractors. He has just started his sponsorship this season. He believes it's good for the company and it also fulfils his long time interest in motorcycling of all kinds. Dean is an ex-bike rider himself. He rode moto-cross for 20 years before he broke his shoulder three years ago, and so started to get involved in speedway through someone he knows, Keith at Rye House. His surfacing business is successful but demanding, so he views sponsorship of Davey, and his recent involvement with speedway, as the ideal antidote to the everyday pressures and stress of his work. Apparently the management of all his vans, lorries and trucks, and the need to ensure that all the construction work was done yesterday, was never quite fully relieved as a keen Watford Football Club season ticket holder. Dean has just started to learn the ropes involved in sponsorship and is Davey's key secondary sponsor. He's still new enough to enjoy the sight his company's initials on Davey Watt's bike cover and upon his race suit where it appears on the arm, leg and epaulette. No one can deny that Dean takes considerable pride in the image Davey projects.

The friendly welcome Dean received at Eastbourne amazed him – from the promotion to the riders themselves – particularly compared to his previous experience as a sponsor, when he tried to gain access to the pits at Poole speedway for whom Davey rode last season. Dean was refused entry to the pits at Poole on the basis that even sponsors that had contributed as much as £25,000 to Tony Rickardsson's campaign apparently didn't expect to receive access. In fairness, access to the pits is a privilege and I'm delighted to have this rare treat at Wolves, thanks to Chris van Straaten and Jon Cook's kind hospitality. On a busy race night, it's the prerogative of any club to determine who has access and if the Poole riders and staff want to be stand-offish and "keep themselves to themselves" that is, ultimately, their choice.

Dean points out that tonight Davey will miss the services of his usual mechanic, his young Australian compatriot and King's Lynn rider, Trevor Harding. Now that Dean draws my attention to this, it's very noticeable that everyone else in the Eagles' pits tries to help Davey get things ready with his bike. As I watched earlier, I could see that each rider had their own individual way to psyche themselves up and mentally prepare for the meeting. The most unique style of preparation belongs to Eastbourne Captain David 'Floppy' Norris who deliberately appeared to try to maintain a rather aloof distance from the clamour of the many fans. Not that he didn't also pose for photos or sign programmes, but his whole body language communicated a reserve that says 'do not interrupt for too long'. Now that he's found his own space, Floppy embarks on a weird series of callisthenics that mostly involves waving his arms around in a vigorous circular manner. It all appears very unorthodox and conducted as if he wants to fly off as much as stretch his arms to prepare for the racing. He does all this in his civilian clothes of jeans, trainers and dark jacket style anorak, before he changes into his kevlars, but throughout he bizarrely wears his racing gloves. All very Alan Partridge 'smart casual'.

Close by to Floppy, Dean 'Deano' Barker appears totally unconcerned or to engage in any form of warm-up exercise while Steen Jensen's routine involves either the melodramatic adjustments to his racing gloves, as though he were a fighter pilot, or alternatively, he strikes the sort of elegant, aerodynamic but completely stationary poses on his bike that you imagine he later hopes to reproduce on the track when his bike is travelling at high speed. Perhaps, it's some advanced form of sports visualisation exercise? Whatever his intentions, for now Steen is content to twist his body into the various shapes required for this simulation, all of which can be accomplished without any need to start his bike.

In contrast, Nicki Pedersen sits quietly, isolated in the far corner of the pits, since he's wholly absorbed in the painstaking and fastidious cleaning of his goggles with some sort of fluid and a cloth. He then takes a similarly deliberate approach to the maintenance of his crash helmet and conducts a close, rigorous inspection of the tear-off's mechanism that is an essential accessory for all contemporary speedway riders. In fact, the highest-level speedway riders have a huge array of paraphernalia that, in the pits during the televised World Championship Grand Prix series, definitely requires that you have many available pegs upon which to rest all four of your brightly shone but differently coloured helmets. It's a milieu that Nicki is familiar with but I can't help but notice the calm quietude of his person, attitude and preparations for this Elite League meeting, which is in sharp contrast to his aggressive on-track persona or public perceptions of his outlook and personality. Nicki then does some serious stretches and other bending exercises that are part of a well-rehearsed routine that slightly interrupts his contemplative and comparatively spiritual manner. His great flexibility isn't something I'd ever considered or appreciated beforehand. I watch him bend and place both of his hands completely flat on the floor; an action that I know from yoga requires great discipline, suppleness and flexibility. This might go some way to explain part of his exceptional ability to remain on the bike, after violent knocks and bumps with other riders or sharp manoeuvres at high speed. That is all part and parcel of his combative race technique. It's a skill all gifted riders have, and they often make it look frighteningly easy and controlled, but it clearly requires great ability allied to dedicated training. He then shatters the impression of Zen calm created by these preparations to have a pee by the adjacent tall hedge before he performs some impressively loud throat noises as a prelude to a brief bout of advanced spitting.

The two-minute warning then sounds for the first race and, as the riders for heat 1 make their way to the start line, the Eastbourne pair for the next race – Watt and Jensen – start to line up on their bikes on the track that runs from behind the pits and the hedge, that Nicki has just decorated, down to the track gate entrance on the second bend. They patiently wait there on their machines, and don't watch the first race but just wait for it to end. They're pushed off towards the track as the other riders, who have just completed the first heat, return to the pits. In fact, David Norris has immediately set a new track record when he convincingly won heat 1, but I remain in ignorance of this fact until after the meeting, solely due to the acoustics of the tannoy system that appears only directed towards the impressively packed crowd of fans on the grandstand terrace. My inability to understand the garbled announcements is a slight disappointment but is more than made up for by my close proximity to the pits and the great view of the entire track from my vantage point on the bend.

The activity is feverish but purposeful in both teams' pits areas. The bikes need adjustment or repair in the short time that remains before they go out for their next race. It's probably an obvious point, but not one that I'd fully appreciated until now, that the riders apparently pay absolutely no attention whatsoever to the race card or the heat and cumulative score in the match programme, except as it applies to their own next race. They have the evidence of their own eyes when it comes to the race order in any heat, though the razzmatazz of Shaun's deliberately bombastic delivery of the exact details of the race results not only can't be heard in the pits but also is mostly irrelevant for the riders. But for all the speedway fans, it's THE essential tool to understand, record and register the events of the meeting. As there is a personal financial incentive I'm pretty confident that each rider will be aware of his own individual score and what is required for their own next race. However, the riders, if sufficiently interested, mostly rely on their mechanics or, most likely, their team mangers to keep them apprised of the cumulative match scores should they feel the need to know. The information they essentially require from the details that each race card lists is very straightforward and basic; the gate they're programmed to race from, their fellow riders and, hopefully from a fan's perspective, the actual tactics that they'll employ together in the race. Especially since it is notionally still a team sport that requires their joint endeavours to ensure success for their side. Still, whomever they hear the news from, it's clear that the riders just concentrate on their bikes and their own race. Anyway, it would be very difficult to ride, and hold onto a pen and programme with their gloves on.

One thing that the riders all pay a lot of attention to, if possible – apart from the attentions of attractive solicitous female fans – is to watch what actually happens during the racing. Or, more accurately, particularly how the track is riding and how that might affect the racing set ups for their own equipment. Wolverhampton, as Jon Cook correctly identified beforehand, is an ideal track to watch the racing and still pay full attention to the rider's equipment in the pits area.

When they're not already on their bikes, the riders from both sides hover by the track fence and watch the action. They stand together in their respective team groups with various others that include sponsors, press, friends and the team managers who clutch their programmes authoritatively. I keep myself to myself and hesitate to interrupt any of the riders or managers. Eastbourne have arrived mob handed in this respect, since both Jon Cook and Trevor Geer share these duties and studiously gawp at their programmes. Steen Jensen actually engages me in a conversation, after he probably mistakes me for someone with a modicum of expertise or insight. He's not the tallest rider ever, but stands by the barrier to peer at the track, dressed in his shale splattered kevlars, before he sagely mentions to me the "funny inside line" they have at Monmore Green that apparently prevents the easy passing of other riders. It didn't seem to hold him back in his first race, when he followed his teammate Davey Watt home for second place in heat 2, but the rumour of its existence clearly bothers and concerns him. Like all sports the mental side is crucial and the diminutive 20-year-old Dane now appears unduly preoccupied with the reputation of this possible impediment to his future success to ever truly regain psychological mastery of the circuit. In order to try to help with some psychology myself and distract him from his continual anxious squinting at the inner ring of the track, I try to boost his nervous if not yet deflated self-esteem, with compliments about his performance so far tonight. As well as the week before, when I saw him ride quickly and frequently pass other riders at Reading for the Isle of Wight in the Premier League. Like here, it was his first visit to that track and his performance showed some pluck and much skill. Slightly morosely, Steen dismisses my encouragement, though he notes, "my gating was shit there". I didn't expect to talk, but throughout our brief encounter Steen comes across as approachable and very modest, albeit with a very fragile confidence in his own abilities.

I stand in the thick of things and it's completely fantastic, although I speak to no one. Stranded at the airport, the absence of the two Swedish riders for Wolves appears to initially make a big difference to Wolves' performance as, after a heat win by Floppy in heat 5, Eastbourne already lead by six points. I continue to watch from my ideal vantage point in front of the pits by the concrete wall that separates the grassy area from the greyhound track, which in turn is separated from the speedway track by a wire safety fence, and the Eastbourne riders frequently join me to watch. Most notably Davey Watt, who spends his time spitting with such violence and frequency that I begin to suspect that he is afflicted with some severe expectoration problem. I later learn that it's a common affliction, since the shale and the dust flies into your mouth with great velocity when you race and can't really be prevented from doing so, even when you lead throughout. I subsequently notice that most riders deliberately cover their mouths before they put on their helmets to race. However, Davey has won one race and only trailed behind Nicki Pedersen who rides far ahead in the distance, as usual eschewing any form of team riding, in the other. So along with the apparent lack of dust because of the earlier intensive watering, it's difficult to see where his early coughing stage of pneumoconiosis has developed.

Even after the earlier extensive watering, the quickly drying and unusual track conditions, in the absence of the forecast rain, also appears to play its part in catching the home side out. Indeed, the earlier decision to over-water the surface has resulted in an extremely grippy track as it dries and, if judged by how the riders race, the inside line appears very bumpy and thereby forces the riders to go out much wider than usual towards the potentially hazardous chain link fence. As on many tracks, the riders seem to hug close to the fence just as they reach their highest speeds on the straights. To the untrained eye this looks somewhat perilous on the tight circuit at Monmore Green, where the chance to unexpectedly catch your footrest in the fence appears to loom at any moment. Whether it's the grippy surface, a footrest in the fence or sheer inexperience is difficult to gauge, but the most junior rider on the night, 16-year-old guest Jack Hargreaves, hits or gets caught in the safety fence during heat 6. The velocity of the crash throws him and his bike dramatically into the air and Steen Jensen, who trailed Hargreaves, makes a full-on impact into the fallen Jack and his bike. The carnage of man and machine causes the race to be stopped in the interests of safety by the referee and Hargreaves is excluded as the primary cause.

There is quite some delay and so I find myself next to Adam Shields to whom I mention that they're taking a long time to restart. A man notoriously of few words, he pauses before he says "yup" in a manner that combines brevity and disdain before he meanders back to the pits to tinker with his bike. It's a sharp contrast to the affable Jensen, who is the first to disentangle himself from the carnage on the track and slowly bob back, albeit gingerly, to the pits. But it's an extremely long time, before Hargreaves moves from where he lies prone on the track surface. There's a large crowd of St John Ambulance staff, track personnel, Peter Adams, and assorted riders in attendance and I'm glad to see that Floppy himself immediately runs over to where the young Hargreaves receives attention. I'm impressed by this gesture of sportsmanship and, afterwards, I notice Floppy speak with Davey Watt's sponsor, Dean Saunders, as he returns to the pits. But then Dean swiftly shatters my illusions when he reports that Floppy had gone over to help them clear the track because he'd suspected that the Wolves' team hoped to possibly rather cynically delay proceedings in the hope of rain. During the delay, I take the opportunity to watch the Wolverhampton pits where the activity and attention they pay to their equipment remains throughout the delay at a feverish pitch for most riders and mechanics. The Eastbourne team appear more confident and laid back in their attitude. I also notice Belle Vue's Joe Screen, reputedly one of the nice guys and one of the most gifted but modest riders of his generation, while he visits all and sundry in the pits on one of his few precious nights off from competitive speedway. This confirms, once again, the easy camaraderie and genuine interest that seems to naturally exist among most of the riders in the sport, that is when they're not racing each against each other. He spends quite some time deep in conversation with a smiling Dean 'Deano' Barker before he follows Top Cat's frequently uttered advice to mingle, mingle, mingle. After a long delay the racing eventually resumes.

Back in the pits while he waits for the re-run, Nicki sits quietly on his stool with his mouth pressed against what looks like a giant hand-held hairdryer. I assume it's some sort of a contraption that delivers pure oxygen. Whatever it does, Nicki sucks on it strongly before he storms to an easy win in the re-run of the race, which the home crowd greets with loud boos and a variety of readily understandable arm gestures. Clearly, the crowd no longer holds him in great affection or high esteem. This doesn't seem to concern Nicki at all, because after every race he's content to sit quietly in the corner of the pits or intermittently suck on his hairdryer, while his mechanics efficiently prepare his bike for its next run. He temporarily breaks off from his studious concentration to exchange a few jovial pleasantries with Joe Screen before he resumes with some fastidious cleaning and preparation of his helmet. On the track, the Wolves have stormed away to win the next heat, in which they used the Tactical Substitute rule to great effect, and so have almost restored the scores to parity. The next heat is shared before Nicki stimulates further ire from the Wolves' fans when he has the temerity to line up at the start gate for his next race. I'm lucky to have a great view of the riders as they leave the start and seek to gain that vital yard as they all enter the first bend. In this race, heat 9, three riders make the start – Johnson, Pedersen and Lindgren – and arrive together almost in a line at the first corner. As they broadside into the bend, they bunch together before the Swede and the Dane find themselves badly tangled together. Pedersen and Lindgren are flung unceremoniously from their machines with great velocity into the inflated cushion of the air fence. It's difficult to judge the exact sequence of events that lead to the crash, but it appeared to me that both riders had ridden aggressively with neither of them prepared to give any quarter, before they both lifted slightly and Pedersen collected Lindgren, who was on his outside since he started from gate 3.

Whatever the exact sequence of events, Lindgren leaps to his feet to gesticulate at Pedersen and to take great exception to his violent introduction to the safety fence. What was a full and frank exchange of views and contrary opinions between the two riders would just have been routine if it had then remained at that level of handbags, after what was definitely a dramatic but, in the normal scheme of things, an unexceptional first-bend racing incident. However, when Nicki Pedersen is involved, it's often handled very differently, as his reputation appears to colour subsequent events and interpretations. So it proves in this instance, because things instantly degenerate when Lindgren decides to throw some punches at Pedersen, which has the effect of instantly summoning an angry pack of riders and mechanics from both teams to the incident. As luck would have it everything happens right in front of me.

A frequent complaint about professional wrestling is that a sport, which appears 'real', is patently fixed. The common complaint about ice-hockey fights is that while the level of aggression and battle is often tremendous, the lack of traction prevents any real damage, although I can't help but think that ice-hockey sticks still hurt. Speedway itself is even sometimes accused or rumoured not to be all that it appears to be. But with regards to this fight at Wolverhampton among the riders and mechanics, I can safely say that this is one of the most extreme few minutes of genuine fighting and real violence that I have ever witnessed first hand. I find this ironic because one of the reasons I am writing the book in the first place is because of the 'family values' that the sport usually enshrines. Well, perhaps it still genuinely harbours these values among the fans but now, among the riders, I'm not so sure as I witness what pure adrenalin and the heat of the moment can unfortunately create.

At its simplest, Lindgren and Pedersen couldn't have been surrounded more quickly by other actual and would-be combatants if you'd offered a million-pound prize for the first 10 arrivals at the scene. Riders and mechanics literally sprint from the pits across the grass to very impressively vault the greyhound wall, safety and air fences to join the fracas in varying degrees. As a team-building exercise for the Eastbourne Eagles it is arguably excellent as, like the three musketeers, it is 'all for one and one for all' when the fists and the boots began to fly. First to the scene and with a great turn of speed for a man of his age, and his usually leisurely demeanour, is the Eagles' co-team manager Trevor Geer. His role of potential peacemaker is short-lived after the simultaneous arrival of the man-mountain figure of the security guard from the Wolves' side of the pits, who is closely accompanied by Lindgren's own mechanic. I initially mistake 'the Hulk' for a person who'd been hired by the Wolves as a security guard to prevent violence and, by his persuasive actions mediate among the combatants, to thereby maintain order at this speedway fixture. But, as it turns out, he is Lindgren's own unhinged avenger and berserker with bulging muscles and a closely shaven head. My transient illusion that he is there to stop trouble is swiftly shattered by his unique approach to mediation; which not only involves some impressive gymnastic skills, that brings him trackside promptly, but also the skilful use of his personal 'mediators' at the end of his arms and legs. Dean Barker, distinctive by his combative attitude and rage-filled features, manages to restrain Lindgren's smaller sized mechanic from inflicting any permanent damage on a helmeted Pedersen by eventually wrestling him to the ground. But a strong desire to intervene and to protect his father from being attacked by the apparently crazed 'security guard', who himself takes offence to Trevor Geer's arrival to intercede between the riders and Lindgren's mechanic, sees Chris 'Geernob' Geer foolhardily throw himself at the Hulk. This despite the huge differences in size, strength and weight that are instantly apparent to the casual observer. Unfortunately, this valour and bravery doesn't really translate into effective action, although it does have the instant effect to switch the Hulk's attention from the father to the son. Without so much as a by-your-leave, the security guard then launches into kicking Geer's unprotected head as he tried to get up from the track, one of the most ferocious and repeated kickings that I have ever had the misfortune to witness. Anywhere, never mind at a speedway meeting! The blows to Geer's head are sickening in their ferocity and even footballs aren't usually kicked that hard. The extreme naked violence of the thug and the bully happens in full force in front of me and everyone else, including the distant but still vociferous Wolves' home crowd on the grandstand terraces.

It's hard for me now to establish the actual order of events or exactly recall all the details, particularly as so much went on so quickly, but it appeared it took an age to restore any semblance of order to the trackside and pits areas. Such a blurry recollection of the exact order and sequence of extreme events is often experienced by the police when they interview victims of violence for a statement, who most often can closely describe the weapon in great detail but not the actual perpetrator.

My impression is that the bystanders on the Eastbourne side are Davey Watt, Steen Jensen and, bizarrely, as the cause of the altercation Nicki

Pedersen. He quickly withdraws from the action. Everyone else from the Eastbourne team joins the mêlée to a greater or lesser degree as well as the subsequent chase around the pits and close to the office area.

My familiarity with the Wolves' team and mechanics isn't comparable, so I can't name them so accurately as I can the Eastbourne riders, nonetheless, some of their riders also definitely take an active role as the disturbance and subsequent chase that spills all over the vicinity of the pits area for the next five or so minutes. At the forefront of the action for the Eagles, though definitely not its instigator, is David Norris along with Dean 'Deano' Barker who throws himself about the place with more gusto and desire that his recent rather tepid performances on the track belied. He is definitely the kind of man you'd like to be on your side in a fight or, in this case, trying to mediate a ferocious fight. Deano throws himself on people much bigger than himself, which is most people, except for other speedway riders or Freddie Lindgren's mechanic who he unhesitatingly tackles to prevent him from landing further punches on Pedersen. This has the effect of momentarily attracting Hulk's attention before he gets down to the serious business of treating Geernob's head as a football. Throughout David 'Floppy' Norris switches from his standard default setting of wry and petulant moodiness to a man seized with an inferno of self-righteous anger. This involves him in some impressive and aggressive finger pointing, much shouting, contorted features, and teeth bared in anger as well as also trying to restrain others. Floppy is also the first and loudest of the pack of Eastbourne staff that chases the Hulk from the scene of the crime, and presumably his employment by the club as a 'security man', through the pits and out of the stadium. [Footnote 4 later in the season, the Hulk is astonishingly spotted in the Wolves' pits.] Again my exact recollection of events is sketchy but after the extreme violence of his assault the Hulk, with the definite assistance of Floppy, decides to make just an even quicker exit than he did on arrival at the crash scene.

Floppy demonstrated a considerable speed on his feet and a voluble but commendable desire to locate a policeman, although he has temporarily forgotten the immutable law that, like London buses, there's never a policeman when you need one and that no amount of shouting will ever help find one. The violent chain of events clearly causes Floppy to forget the famed ethos that speedway prides itself on, namely that it never requires the attendance of police or stewards to marshal or separate groups of fans that you often find essential at other sports. And so he runs round frantically at high speed, shouty and, at times, almost manic in his fruitless search for the law. The closest person to a legal representative available is the match official Chris Durno, in the role of judge, jury and peacemaker, who swiftly arrives from the referee's box. Chris who, by the time he reaches the pits to restore good order, has substantial confusion to mediate with all agitated and loudly shouting people, who all immediately claim to be the injured or slighted party.

The reactions of the management of both sides are interesting and instructive. Trevor Geer, for such an apparently taciturn and mild-mannered man, quickly runs to the initial incident but after that refrains from further involvement, though his son ensures the Geers remained well represented. Jon Cook tries to act as a peacemaker throughout, but also chases around madly with Floppy and Deano in hot pursuit of the perpetrator and the subsequent fruitless hunt for assistance from the absent long arm of the law. Lindgren's mechanic sparked the whole incident by his initial decision to intervene on the track and attempt to twat Pedersen. The incredible fighting machine from 'security' displayed a huge capacity for extreme violence matched only by his ability to scarper with the lightning speed of Ben Johnson when Floppy demanded legal retribution from the boys in blue. However, his turn of speed had nothing on that shown by Chris van Straaten who disappeared into his office with an alacrity that must be useful during the emergency evacuation of an aeroplane. They say when the going gets tough the tough get going and Chris immediately got going, albeit back to his own office. The speed with which he removed himself from the scene would have severely restricted his ability to have an informed opinion of what happened based on the evidence of his own eyes. Though he is one of the most experienced, influential and respected members of the speedway's hierarchy and governing body, it's still bound to disappoint when the action moves to within yards of his office, definitely within his jurisdiction, and he simply disappears in a 'now you see him now you don't' type manner, albeit without the obligatory wisp of smoke. Perhaps he'd already gone to look for the large carpet to privately sweep the whole incident under that both clubs and the SCB would require later. From his television appearances, Peter Adams strikes me as man very much in control of himself and his reaction to things that happen around him, though he also impresses you as someone you wouldn't like to mess with verbally or physically. During and afterwards, wearing his distinctive, bright old gold and black coloured Wolverhampton jacket, he didn't seem that ruffled or upset. They say when all around you lose their heads that it's best to keep your own, which Peter does with some assurance. He appears unconcerned at the absence of law enforcement officers when Floppy angrily requests such assistance from him and also phlegmatically confirms the impressively clean pair of heels shown by the departed assailant, when the Eagles' staff demand that he be found and lynched for his actions. That said Peter had earlier shown himself to be in control of his public demeanour even when annoyed and this approach serves him well in the aftermath of the fight, when he appears simultaneously nonchalant and unconcerned. But then the Wolves' riders and staff would expect him to publicly represent their best interests in every conceivable situation. That said Peter also strikes me as the sort of man who would frankly let you have his opinions afterwards in private. That night he demonstrates his experience, when he skilfully and methodically channels the waves of annoyance and anger that surround this situation, never mind the disadvantageous absence of his Swedish riders, to positive effect for his team.

Chris Durno then summons the teams and their managers to the equivalent of a post-coital cigarette in the form of a confidential dressing down. He administers this during an earlier than anticipated interval break to allow everyone the chance to calm down before the re-run of the race resumed the fixture. However, on the grandstand terraces, the milk of human kindness doesn't course quickly through the veins of the enraged Wolves' faithful when it comes to forgiving Nicki Pedersen or indeed forgetting the supposedly barbaric transgressions of their Public Enemy Number 1. The fact that Nicki sits quietly and calmly on his stool in his corner of the away pits, hairdryer-shaped ventilator in hand while he patiently shines his goggles, further inflames feelings of outrage. So much so that many of the visiting fans feel the force of these objections to such an extent that some of them seek protection and make a tactical retreat to the safety of the normally closed grassy areas by the pits.

My proximity to the away pits area allows me to watch Nicki Pedersen nonchalantly wait for the end of the enforced early interval. He also takes the opportunity to remind his mechanics and teammates to focus on the job in hand and rallies them with a shout of "hey, boys; forget about it, let's get ready!" The re-run of heat 9 sees Denmark's very own version of Danger Mouse greeted with loud boos and a variety of insults and gestures by the start line, whereas Freddie Lindgren is lauded with similar vigour through noisy cheers and applause, almost as loud as the jeers for Pedersen. Lindgren seems determined to prove his worth on the track and victory appears to be within his grasp when he overtakes Pedersen on the third bend of the last lap. But, instead, Pedersen uses his undoubted skill and determination in combination with the track knowledge he has gained through his time spent with Wolves, to just sneak a deserved victory right at the finish line. It's a win that he definitely relishes and he celebrates with a brief onanist gesture to the loudly aggrieved hordes of disappointed Wolves' fans. Watt and Shields then combine for a 4–2 heat victory in the next race to extend Eastbourne's slight lead to three points with five races left. I watch the next heat beside the very affable Steen Jensen, who seems nonplussed at the need we have in this country to fight over something as silly as a speedway race. His only comment on the incident, "freaking Swedes", reflects the traditional Danish antipathy towards Sweden as much as what actually happened. Steen is keen to emphasise that he'd never fight and already looks forward to when the fixture is over so he can practise his skills and riding technique elsewhere on some of the country's larger tracks. Trevor Geer and Peter Adams now make a point to take the time to be seen to chat as normal between the races. This is still the basic appeal of the sport where no quarter is given on the track but, mostly, everyone remains firm friends off it. In fact, everything seems to have returned to normal in both pits except for Deano who sits by himself and looks very thoughtful and disconsolate, as he stares at his gloved hands. Earlier he'd been zealous as he defended his own corner and that of his teammates during the melee – which he'd instantly joined as he attempted to throw punches and hold much bigger people than himself back or restrain the wildly flailing Lindgren – but now he looks exhausted and almost depressed. His two races that, so far, haven't troubled the scorer can't help his apparently sour outlook.

A few minutes later, as we watch Eastbourne get another 3–3 to retain their slender lead, I find myself with Jon Cook who also looks far from happy. In this race Floppy finally finishes a comfortable second, but not before an unforced error costs him the lead that has him eventually finish behind David Howe. Even though I have watched many races, I have no idea why he made this unfortunate manoeuvre until Jon remarks matter of factly, "he was going too fast to try to cut back like that". It's amazing what experienced and tutored eyes can spot that the fans like myself won't see at all. As the riders approach the tapes for heat 12, Jon goes out of his way to sincerely apologise for his invitation that led me to attend this particularly stormy meeting as his guest and that of the Eastbourne club. Jon persists with his apologies, "I'm sorry that you had to witness that" before he sighs and continues with "I would have loved all that in the old days but I'm really getting too old for that now!" I complement his team and staff, since they clearly stuck together and showed their resilience in the face of perceived external threats. It's just the sort of spirit that you'd want in your team, especially when so many of the top Elite league riders only briefly travel into the country for a meeting before they immediately leave again to ride for one of their many other speedway teams. Such camaraderie has a rather old-fashioned quality and the willingness to look after your colleagues is the sort of behaviour that you often pay expensive consultants to try to pretend to instil in your staff in normal business life.

The result of the next race doesn't improve Jon's outlook because Deano and Davey Watt return to the pits after they finish a considerable distance behind the Wolves' riders for a 5–1 result that concedes the overall lead 38–37. The apparent newly confirmed but found in adversity team spirit then crashes spectacularly in a loud, blazing argument between the two riders. They say it takes to two to tango or to argue, but Deano is quite happy to conduct the argument with little or no response from Davey Watt except for the occasional word. Not that this lack of response stops Deano, who hurls any of his racing gear that is to hand around the pits and repeats, in no uncertain terms, his dissatisfaction with Davey's abilities, team riding skills or overall spatial awareness on the track. Rather than intervene Jon Cook exasperatedly remarks, "I'm just not listening to this!" before he walks away. The argument eventually blows out in the face of the limited response from Watt to Deano's considerable display of contempt and ire. Glenn, Deano's mechanic, shrugs when I mention that his boss doesn't seem too happy with things before he notes, "it doesn't help that he's riding very poorly at the moment; he's only got seven points in three meetings". Davey Watt's sponsor, Dean, spends the next little while in conversation with him as he prepares for his next race, when he'll partner his less volatile fellow countryman Adam Shields. Afterwards, Dean complains, "Barker just doesn't have the right attitude".

Someone who does have the right attitude by almost any estimation, or at least considerable determination, is Nicki Pedersen who celebrates with another win in a rather pressured but vital heat 13. The crowd boos him before and afterwards, which he repays in kind with wild but rude gestures of celebration. The next heat is drawn to set up this contest up for a thrilling last heat finale. Again Pedersen storms to a victory that, once more, he celebrates with that distinctive but joyfully delivered gesture to the crowd. The Eastbourne riders then proceed onto their victory parade. The lap of honour provides another chance for the Wolves' fans assembled on the grandstand terrace to rush forward to better vent their considerable frustration at the outcome of this fixture. The Eastbourne riders smile and wave even more exuberantly in response to this very public display of aggrieved disgruntlement. As soon as they return to the pits, the victory smiles quickly fade as they're immediately called away by an extremely stern Jon Cook to their dressing room for an urgent team meeting. Suddenly the Eastbourne side of the pits is totally deserted and the tension of the evening still hangs in the atmosphere, albeit without any of the key protagonists present. By the time I find my way back through the crowds that still throng from the pits area to the track shop, the consensus among the home support appears to be that if only their Swedish riders could have organised their travel properly, they'd have won the fixture easily. As it was, on the night, their nemesis was Nicki Pedersen and he made all the difference in the final 46–47 score line when he rode unbeaten in all five of his races. Dave and John in the track shop feel that it's typical of Wolves to get so close without actually being able to supply the required metaphorical killer blow, no matter how literally they tried to land actual blows earlier in the meeting!

2nd May 2005 Wolves v Eastbourne (Elite League A) 46–47

Postscript from *When Eagles Dared*

The meeting eventually came down to a last heat decider, held in a decidedly tense atmosphere that Nicki coolly ignored (as he had studiously done all night when sat calmly alone in his own section of the pits) to complete his five ride, 15-point maximum. He celebrated wildly to loud jeers from the Monmore faithful and replied to their unmistakeable gestures in reciprocal fashion. After a warmly serenaded victory parade for the Eagles from the Monmore faithful, they retreated to their dressing rooms for a lengthy team talk behind closed doors with Jon Cook.

The SCB had to order an extra large carpet under which to hide the results of its subsequent enquiry into the events of the night. No details were ever publicly released – though I understand both clubs received fines – and the speedway world continued in its orbit, just as it always had, in its own sweet way. The Matrix reasserted itself and the speedway press, the local media and the Internet forums buzzed with claim, counterclaim and outlandish supposition. Photos that incriminated both sides were published that showed conflicting images of the fracas, though some of these mysteriously and quickly disappeared. Wolverhampton and Eastbourne promised their full co-operation with the authorities.

The Wolves official website commented:

"Tempers boiled over following a first bend tangle between Lindgren and Nicki Pedersen in Heat 9, with representatives from both clubs involved in some unsavory scenes. Referee Chris Durno called an early interval and restored order, and the action which followed was out of the top drawer."

Whereas the Eagles official website noted with a firmly pointed finger:

"We will cooperate fully with any investigation and would like to place on record our support for the actions of the match referee in difficult circumstances. We would like to state our shock and outrage at the actions of a member of the Wolverhampton speedway security team and trust that the appropriate actions will be taken by his employer … The catalyst to the whole incident, a Wolverhampton Speedway Mechanic, was dealt with by the Referee on the night, and we trust that once Wolverhampton speedway have acted against their Security steward, both teams can move on and enjoy successful seasons"

If this were *Dixon of Dock Green*, as soon as was seemly after the denouement, Jack Warner always appeared just before the screen fades to black to wrap up and then say "good night all". Though, significantly in a break with tradition, for once he wouldn't update us on what happened to the so-called culprits. Again idle speculation about what has or hasn't happened is no basis for further comment on my part. In my previous account of these events in my book *Showered in Shale* Jon Cook asked a rhetorical question for which the answer is thankfully, most of the time, "speedway". The question was, "in what other sport could participants be assaulted by the staff employed by the home team and the police not become involved?"